Hoi An Travel Guide, Vietnam

Tourism Information

Author
David Mills.

SONITTEC PUBLISHING. All rights reserved. No part of this publication may be reproduced, distributed, or transmitted in any form or by any means, including photocopying, recording, or other electronic or mechanical methods, without the prior written permission of the publisher, except in the case of brief quotations embodied in critical reviews and certain other noncommercial uses permitted by copyright law. For permission requests, write to the publisher, addressed "Attention: Permissions Coordinator," at the address below.

Copyright © 2019 Sonittec Publishing
All Rights Reserved

First Printed: 2019.

ISBN:

Publisher:
SONITTEC
2162 Davenport House
261 Bolton Road
Bury
Gtr. Manchester
BL8 2NZ
United Kingdom

Table of Content

SUMMARY	1
HOI AN INTRODUCTION	4
TRAVEL AND TOURISM	9
TOP THINGS TO DO	16
Beaches	16
An Bang Beach	16
Cua Dai Beach	18
Hiking, walking tours and itineraries	20
Do-it-yourself photo tour	20
Self-guided tour of Hoi An's old town	21
Exploring by bike or motorbike	23
Historic attractions	24
The Ba Le Well	24
Temples	26
Van Duc Pagoda	26
Chuc Thanh Pagoda	28
Phuoc Lam Pagoda	29
Shopping	30
Tailoring	32
General activities	34
Cam Kim and other islands	34
Hoi An for families	36
Food tours	38
Day trips	40
Lang Co	40
Cham Island	42
My Son	44
The Ho Chi Minh Trail with Hoi An Motorbike Adventures	46
Yoga	50
Festivals and events	52
Full moon lantern festival	52
Mid-Autumn Festival	54
Cooking classes	57
Cultural areas	59
Thanh Ha Pottery Village	59

Where to stay in Hoi An 62
Hoi An old town 67
- Almanity 69
- Orchids Homestay 70
- Anantara Hoi An Resort 72
- Cozy Hoian Villas 74
- La Residencia 75
- Strawberry Garden Homestay 76
- Thien Nga Hotel 77
- Vinh Hung 1 Heritage Hotel 79
- Vinh Hung Library Hotel 81
- Ha An Hotel 83
- Hoang Trinh Hotel 84
- Like Hoi An Hotel 85
- Thien Thanh Boutique Hotel 87
- Tribee Hostel 89
- Vesper Homestay 91
- Volar Homestay 92

An Hoi islet 93
- Lantana Boutique Hotel 93
- Phong Le Villa Hostel 95

An Bang Beach 97
- Christina's Hoi An 97
- Red Flower Cottage Homestay 98
- An Bang Seaside Village 100
- An Bang Sunset Village Homestay 101
- Nhu Que Vegetable Village Homestay 103
- The Hippie House 105
- Under the Coconut Tree Homestay 106
- An Bang Garden Homestay 108

Cua Dai Beach 109
- Victoria Hoi An Beach Resort & Spa 110

Cua Dai Street 113
- Hoi An Ancient House Village Resort & Spa 113
- Paddy's Hostel 115
- Rock Villa Hoi An 117
- Muca Boutique Resort 119
- Villa Hoa Su -- Frangipani Village Resort 121

- Cham Island 123
  - Hammock Homestay or Dich Vu Luu Tru Cai Vong 124
- QUICK GUIDE 126
  - Getting in 126
  - Get around 134
  - Seeing 138
  - Doing 146
  - Spa 156
  - Cooking Class 157
  - Learn 157
  - Buying 159
  - Eating 173
  - Drink 195

Summary

The world is a book and those who do not travel read only one page.

It is indeed very unfortunate that some people feel traveling is a sheer waste of time, energy and money. Some also find traveling an extremely boring activity. Nevertheless, a good majority of people across the world prefer traveling, rather than staying inside the confined spaces of their homes. They love to explore new places, meet new people, and see things that they would not find in their homelands. It is this very popular attitude that has made tourism, one of the most profitable, commercial sectors in the world.

People travel for various reasons. Some travel for work, others for fun, and some for finding mental peace. Though every person may have his/her own reason to go on a journey, it is essential to note that traveling, in itself, has some inherent advantages. For one, for some days getting away from everyday routine is a pleasant change. It not only refreshes one's body, but also mind and soul. Traveling to a distant place and doing exciting things that are not thought of otherwise, can rejuvenate a person, who then returns home, ready to take on new and more difficult challenges in life and work. It makes a person forget his worries, problems, frustrations, and fears, albeit for some time. It gives him a chance to think wisely and constructively. Traveling also helps to heal; it can mend a broken heart.

For many people, traveling is a way to attain knowledge, and perhaps, a quest to find answers to their questions. For this, many people prefer to go to faraway and isolated places. For believers, it is a search for God and to gain higher knowledge; for others, it is a search for inner peace. They might or might not find what they are looking for, but such an experience certainly enriches their lives

David Mills

Hoi An Introduction

Most travellers will rate Hoi An close to the top of their list of places to visit in Vietnam. It's a perfect combination of history, architecture, cuisine and beaches. And then there's the shopping.

Hoi An's World Heritage listed old streets have been overrun with tailors, trinket vendors, galleries and restaurants all vying for the traveller dollar. And few travellers leave without obliging them. Foreign trade has been the lifeblood of this town for centuries and Hoi An's tourism onslaught has continued the tradition.

Looking back
Hoi An's days as a trading port date back a few millenia. The Cham people who controlled central and southern Vietnam for more than a millenia, established

a lucrative spice trade here. But the southward thrust of the Viet people in the 15th century crushed the Cham kingdom and saw the establishment of a Vietnamese trading town - Hoi An - that flourished through to the early 19th century.

Hoi An's heyday brought lucrative trade from China, Japan as well as Europe. And treasure for trade was not the only thing to arrive. French Jesuit missionary Alexandre de Rhodes also added Hoi An to his destination for spreading the faith.

Not content with proselytising, de Rhodes mastered the Vietnamese language and created a new Romanised script from its Chinese based characters. His Romanised system, known as quoc ngu, was later mandated by French colonial authorities as the official written form of the Vietnamese language and it is this script that is used in modern Vietnam.

The original script, "nom" while still visible at historic sites throughout the country, is now out of use and only understood by a small number of scholars.

In the late nineteenth century Hoi An's Thu Bon River silted up making it impassable for commercial shipping. The port moved to Tourane - now Danang - and Hoi An languished. Its retreat into small town anonymity meant that its old buildings survived the joint ravages of war and development. The beautifully preserved town that has been at the heart of Vietnam's tourism revival is once again a commercial centre, the air crowded with spruiking and foreign languages.

If the destruction of heritage in other Vietnamese cities and towns is anything to go by, the world can be grateful for Hoi An's World Heritage designation. It has put rigid controls around any changes to the old town. Locals have come to appreciate the value of the tourism dollar and seem content that their town will be prosperous even if it never experiences a building binge of the kind that has shaped most of the country's urban areas.

Hoi An's old town is small and quaint and the absence of cars from its historic streets make it a wonderful place to spend slow time - eat, walk, cycle and explore. You won't need our encouragement to shop.

Cao lau and other local culinary specialties are delicious, accessible and available everywhere. And some of Vietnam's best cooking classes are run here.

Many of the old houses and pagodas are open for visitors using a strangely complicated ticketing system. While the history is rarely more than token, these old merchant homes and places of worship are very interesting.

Nearby, a visit to the Cham ruins at My Son is worthwhile and a cycle around Cam Kim Island on the Thu Bon River is a delight.

Divers and snorkellers also flock to daily boat trips exploring the coral and marine life off nearby Cham Island.

Travel and Tourism

Tourism is now Hoi An's bread and butter but the town's rise began thanks to international trade. With an ideal position in the delta of the lower Thu Bon River bordering the sea, Hoi An was a traffic hub, connecting both domestic markets and international trade routes. In its heyday in the early 17th century, it was one of the busiest commercial ports in Southeast Asia.

Hoi An's origins can be traced back nearly two millennia to Sa Huynh culture pre-second century BC, before it became an important port for the Champa Kingdom from the second to the 15th century. The commercial port was built in the 15th and 16th centuries as traders began to move silk, china, pottery, aloe-wood and swallow's nests to East Asia, Southeast Asia, India and as far as Europe; ships from Spain, Portugal, Holland, France and England anchored for four to six months every year to trade.

The Nguyen Lords allowed the Chinese and Japanese to open shops, build streets and keep their customs. In the 17th century there was a Chinese town, a Japanese town and a Dutch trading port. Hoi An was a confluence where East met West, paving the way for the spread of modern languages, Christianity and Buddhism in Vietnam.

Today the town has 1,107 timber-frame buildings. Pagodas, assembly halls, clan houses and 200-year-old shophouses line the ancient streets. You'll see how buildings connect Nguyen Thai Hoc Street (the front of house serving as the shopfront) to the riverbank making for easy transfer of goods from ships. A big part of the visitor experience is simply strolling the laneways, popping into old buildings, cycling along riverbanks and enjoying the ambience of it all. Heritage sights within the historic quarters require a 120,000 dong ticket that gives entrance to any five places.

Of course, Hoi An didn't earn its reputation among the travellers of today as a must-go just for old buildings. There are endless opportunities for fun.

The town may have declined as a commercial port in the 19th century, but today it thrives on tailoringevery other shop offers you the opportunity to make custom clothes, be it a copy of a favourite dress or a flashy one-of-a-kind zoot suit. It's a fun but slippery slope: go into a shop to browse and emerge with a maxed out credit card and a whole new wardrobe including a skin-tight silk Vietnamese ao dai dress (a word of caution: those dresses accentuate every lump and bump). The number of tailor shops is overwhelming and it may surprise you to know that the majority of those "tailor" shops are just storefronts, with the actual sewing outsourced to workshops.

You may actually need to get new clothes made in order to deal with your expanding waistline; Hoi An is famous for its food. From mobile carts to upscale restaurants, it is a fabulously cheap food-lovers heaven and there is a list of must-tries: cao lau, mi quang, white rose dumplings, Hoi An wontons, chicken rice and quite possibly the best banh mi in Vietnam. Who knew a sandwich could be so magical. Cooking classes and food tours are plentiful.

Part of what makes Hoi An so likeable is the balance it strikes between culture, activity, urban, countryside and beach. Did your ears perk up at the word "beach"? An easy bike ride from town is one very fine beach called An Bang. During the dry season it's tough to pull yourself away from this pretty stretch of sand and water. Bask on a sunbed, lounge at one of the laidback eateries or dig into some of Hoi An's best seafood. Beach bums will also love to hear that An Bang boasts excellent affordable accommodation just a hop from the sand. Once a main attraction, Cua Dai Beach now suffers from severe coastal erosion. However, head to the part in between Cua Dai and An Bang for fantastic undeveloped beach with no crowds. Upping the ante is Cham Island, which boasts even more spectacular sand and water. Join a dive trip or do an overnight stay, braving the unruly public supply boat.

The options are endless and independent travellers find it hard to leave. There's picturesque countryside and many islands to be explored by bicycle, motorbike or boat. Snap those rice paddy pics, paddle in a basket boat down riverways lined with water coconut palms. Further afield, do a day trip to the temple ruins of My Son, one of the most significant Cham sites in Vietnam.

Get your fill of the big city with a daytrip to Da Nang just 30 kilometres northwest along the coast or a motorbike cruise along the famous Hai Van Pass, now a backpacker rite of passage. At the end of the day, make sure there's room on your memory card for a sunset boat ride on the river. At night, meanwhile, the town is a visual feast of colourful lanterns and tourists flock to the river to send candlelit paper lanterns down the water. At the risk of being a wet blanket, the river really doesn't need any more rubbish in it, but if you must buy a lantern, don't buy it from a child and negotiate the price down to 10,000 dong for one. And if you get a tale from the seller about how they struggle to make a living, do know that they actually make a killing.

Yes, Hoi An is a tourist trap and it suffers from its own success. New hotels and homestays continue to spring up, coach buses continually arrive and unleash swarms and at times the selfie-stick wielding crowds can be insufferable. Unlike Luang Prabang, another heritage town often compared to Hoi An, few locals still live within the historic centre. Accommodation is more expensive than other tourist destinations in Vietnam, service can be apathetic and backpackers will struggle to find decent hostels close to the historic quarter. There are three prices to everything: local, Vietnamese

tourist and foreign tourist. Bargaining skills are a must -
- and beware of scams.

Love it or hate it, the old world Hoi An evokes is unlike anything else in a country obsessed with building a new, modern, flashy future.

Top things to do

Beaches

An Bang Beach

Just four kilometres from Hoi An's UNESCO World Heritage centre and 30 kilometres from Da Nang International Airport, An Bang Beach is the perfect complement to the sightseeing and tourist bustle of town. With the once popular Cua Dai Beach suffering from severe erosion, An Bang now holds the crown as Hoi An's go-to beach. Whether you want to hide under an sun umbrella (there are many available), hang out at one the casual bars or plop yourself on white sand, reserve at least a day on your Hoi An itinerary for some An Bang R&R.

The best time to be at An Bang is dry season, which falls between March and September. During this time you can expect blistering sun, soaring temperatures and calm waters. For the price of drink, you can use a restaurant's sun lounger for the day. During the

Vietnamese summer holiday months of June to August, the local Vietnamese crowd flood in for sunrise swims and sunset family beach barbecues.

Cold, wet season lasts from around October to February. The weather definitely puts a dampener on things the ocean is rough and temperatures can be downright bone chilling, though there are surprises with the odd sunny day. Eateries remain open and the beach can still be an incredible place to sit and watch the storms come in over the mountains at the edge of Da Nang. Those six-foot waves also mean that surfers can have some fun.

To get to An Bang from Hoi An town centre, head north on Hai Ba Trung Street. It's four kilometres to the coast. Upon arrival you'll come to an area with various parking lots; expect to pay up to 10,000 dong per motorbike. This area also has plenty of meter taxis waiting use a green Mailinh Taxi. Plan to use one if you want a late night, as it's not ideal to ride your bicycle back to town

Cua Dai Beach

Once the darling of Hoi An, known for its stunning palm-fringed white sand, views of the Cham islands and lux resorts, Cua Dai beach is now affected by severe coastal erosion. Though the erosion has been detected since 2004, the condition has accelerated in recent years.

Cua Dai Beach is located at the end of predictably named Cua Dai Road, running for eight kilometres along the coast, from the tip at the Cham Island ferry port north to An Bang Beach. At the public section the first part you see where Cua Dai Road meets the beach there are parts where it is impossible to take a "walk on the beach" without being waist deep in the ocean. This main hub, with its many seafood restaurants and sun chair rentals, used to be the main draw. Now it is an unsightly disaster/construction zone, a mix of sand bags, tarps, metal sheet piles, ropes and bamboo, and business has all but dried up.

As for the resorts, they have constructed their own protective rock walls and breakwaters. These aren't the most natural sight but they are certainly more attractive than sandbags. If your main purpose of staying at a resort is for the beach, this is not the place. High-end hotels on Cua Dai still deliver on the ocean views, swimming pool, restaurants and services everything but sand between your toes and in your bikini bottoms. If you appreciate amenities and finery, you can get great value as rates have dropped over the years and there are discounts to be had. We continue to recommend Victoria Hoi An Beach Resort & Spa, which does have an adjacent patch of sand complete with loungers.

Is it worth visiting Cua Dai? There are still plenty of seafood places where you can eat and drink yourself silly in between swimming and lounging in the sun and not surprisingly, these places are desperate for business.

Hiking, walking tours and itineraries

Do-it-yourself photo tour

Hoi An is as photogenic as it gets. To help you make the most of Hoi An's picture-perfect charms, here are some tips on getting an album full of great shots. Get those memory cards ready.

The historic town is normally crawling with tourists and it's hard to take a photo without someone else's selfie stick in the way. But the town is blissfully quiet early in the morning, before 07:00. It's the calm before the storm: tour groups have yet to arrive, streets are empty and shops are slowly awakening from their slumber. This is when you can take a picture of that canary yellow building blanketed in pink bougainvillea and bathed in gentle light. Get into those narrow side lanes, get out of the tourist centre and you'll discover that working Hoi An has been going full throttle since dawn. Locals will be slurping up bowls of noodle soup, sipping Vietnamese coffee and delivering kids to school. Head out there and you'll capture some great street food and street scenes.

Markets always make for interesting sights, be it a colourful fruit and vegetable still life or a shot of bustling activity don't get in the way of the deliveries! Hoi An's main market is packed with seven-pigs-on-a-motorbike photo opportunities.

Taking photos of people takes some delicacy how would you like it if you were going about your business and someone stuck a lens in your face? Or photographed your child? Developing a rapport with someone is important, not only so you know it's okay to take a photograph, but also for the subject to warm up to you. The same applies to water buffalo -- sure, they are cute but they frighten easily.

Self-guided tour of Hoi An's old town

An entrance ticket for the sights within the UNESCO World Heritage old town is required. Here's how we'd suggest approaching the various things to see.

Inscribed by UNESCO in 1999, Hoi An "is an exceptionally well-preserved example of a South-East Asian trading port dating from the 15th to the 19th century... The town reflects a fusion of indigenous and foreign cultures (principally Chinese and Japanese with later European influences) that combined to produce this unique survival." What you see today is a townscape built during the 17th and 18th centuries, which still includes 1,107 timber-frame buildings and a street plan that once allowed customer access from the front of them, and convenient off-loading of goods from boats on the river.

The entrance ticket is technically required to enter the old town, but really it is only checked when you go inside one of the 22 buildings or points of interest on the list. The ticket is 120,000 dong, with tear-off coupons allowing entrance to five places. It's valid for 24 hours, though the time period seems to be somewhat flexible. The ticket seller assured us we could use it for our entire stay, be it days or weeks.

Exploring by bike or motorbike

Hoi An's flat but varied countryside makes it an ideal place to jump on a pushbike or motorbike and explore. Pedal down narrow alleys past 18th-century shophouses, wheel through rice fields and along rivers to roads that skirt the beach.

Renting a bicycle is an excellent way to get around as it's cheap and easy to park. Hostels and hotels often include free bicycle or a rental for next to nothing and they are allowed within the historic quarters; motorbikes are not. Those with motorbikes must pay to park at the edge of the town centre.

It's also a very flat, straightforward journey to An Bang and Cua Dai beaches. However, cycling can be a misery in the hot season or midday sun and you can tick off a lot more sights with a motorbike. Rentals cost as little as US$5 but do check on the condition of the bike before you set out. Hoi An traffic moves at a more relaxed and easy pace than big cities like Da Nang, however, if you've never driven a motorbike before, a vacation in Vietnam shouldn't be your first time.

Motorbike helmets are mandatory by law, no matter how short the distance or how good your hair looks. It's considered very poor form for men to ride around without a shirt or women in bikini tops (plus, anything is better than nothing when it comes to road rash protection.

Historic attractions

The Ba Le Well

Of the 80 or so ancient wells located in Hoi An, Ba Le Well is the most well known because it was once considered key to the town's signature cao lau noodle. Thought to have been built in the 10th century by the Cham people, an entire mythology has blossomed around the well, with fanciful stories of mystical connections and fairies.

Ba Le Well is located down the alley running north behind 45 Phan Chai Trinh Street, just up from the popular and tasty Ba Le Well Restaurant. Once a hard to find spot, now you can't miss the easy-to-see UNESCO sign.

Ba Le Well is looked after by Mr Ba Lo Le, a rather ancient, and maybe a little away-with-the-fairies himself guardian who plunged (sorry) all his money into restoring the well. Every day Mr Ba Lo Le takes the water from the well and delivers it to poor families nearby, who use the sacred water for making tea and cooking traditional medicinal watercress soup xi ma, which without this special well water is said to be tasteless.

One family we spoke to tried to convince us that the keeper of the well was almost as old as the well itself, with the strong medicinal powers of the water and its spirits acting as a youthful elixir to keeping him strong and healthy even at the ripe old age of 10,054.

It seems that the Ba Le Well water's use in the cao lau noodle has been put on hold for now, as the Ngoc family -- the only family in town holding the recipe for the noodle and who are responsible for supplying the whole town each day -- have now built their own well to save them time. From this well springs a similar alum-rich water, which they mix with ash, said to give the noodle its chewy texture.

Is the well worth seeking out? Well, only if you are passing by, perhaps as a diversion on your way to chow down at Ba Le Well Restaurant. Time your visit right and you may bump into Mr Ba Lo Le -- at around 15:00 or at dawn -- and meet one of the real characters of Hoi An. He may share a little of his own medicinal tipple, which almost certainly does not come

Temples

Van Duc Pagoda

Van Duc, one of the largest pagodas in Hoi An, is home to monks who are sometimes happy to give you a quick tour of the pagoda and its grounds.

When we visited in May 2016, a large, slick main temple hall was under construction and though built with wood in a traditional style, we wonder if some of the original crumbly charm of this pagoda has been lost.

The best time to visit is in the evening on full moons and auspicious Buddhist celebrations like Buddha's birthday, when monks travel for miles to pray at the pagoda. If you turn up at around 19:00 on these occasions you'll be met by monks weaving their way down through the paddy to the river to release paper lanterns while chanting prayers.

Otherwise, the pagoda can be a pleasant diversion on the way to An Bang Beach (but please, definitely no beach wear!). It's four kilometres from An Bang. If you are travelling north to the beach on Hai Ba Trung, just before the last bridge is the islet with Tra Que vegetable village. Head west from the village for 1.8 kilometres.

Alternatively, if you are travelling from town, travel west on Nguyen Tat Thanh Street. You'll pass the bus station at the corner of Le Hong Phong. From this intersection it is one kilometre until you hit a set of traffic lights at the small intersection with Nguyen Chi Thanh Street. We noticed a sign pointing out the direction of the pagoda "Chua Van Duc" but it was partially obscured and not very noticeable. Turn right here and follow the road straight to the very end, where it snakes off to the right, approximately two kilometres. The gates are on the right hand side.

Chuc Thanh Pagoda

Originally founded in 1454 by Minh Hai, a Chinese Buddhist Monk, this makes Chuc Thanh Pagoda Hoi An's oldest temple. If there is one temple to visit in Hoi An, this is it. The beautiful ancient gateway is still standing, and seeing this alone is worth the journey to the outskirts of the town centre.

A large modern gate has been built in front of it and on the left you'll see three newer pagodas. There's also an extensive cemetery plot to the right that you can wander through. The temple contains antique gongs which are said to be more than 200 years old. The shady, peaceful property is pleasant to stroll around.

Chuc Thanh is easy to find. Travel west on Ly Thuong Kiet Street, which becomes Nguyen Tat Thanh Street. A block past Hai Ba Trung Street, turn right/head north on Tran Van Du Street until the end.

Chuc Thanh is 500 metres from Phuoc Lam Pagoda so it makes sense to see them together. From Chuc Thanh, simply head west on Ton Duc Thang Street, and turn right/go north on Le Hong Phong Street.

Phuoc Lam Pagoda

Phuoc Lam is a beautiful and elaborate temple with many different renderings of the Buddha, including a gold-covered "Buddha as a boy". This is a working temple and is home to a large group of monks.

There's plenty to wander around and look at here, but if you really want to understand it all, go with a good guide.

If you're going on your own, we found it's best to visit just before 11:00 when the monks are finishing up their lunch (they've been up since 04:00 and this is their last meal of the day), after which they line up and circle through the temple, chanting midday prayers.

Phuoc Lam is located on Le Hong Phong, just north of Ton Duc Thang Street. It's set back a bit from the corner. The temple is located only 500 metres from Chuc Thanh Pagoda, so you can easily combine and visit both.

Shopping

Visitors: load up on dong, as there are plenty of things that will catch your eyes when it comes to shopping in Hoi An. How can you resist a conical hat or a tailored shiny zoot suit? Hoi An has everything you never knew you wanted.

Hoi An is known for tailoring but there is enticing ready-made wear as well. Nothing declares that you've been to Vietnam more than pun-tastic, inside-joke T-shirts sporting "Pho-king", "iPho" or "Pho Metal Jacket". For something a little more stylish, find stretchy cotton T-shirts with graphic prints at Ginkgo. Women can head to Metiseko, which specialises in silk clothing and accessories in soft colours and patterns. In other shops, be wary of claims that scarves, clothes and sleeping bag liners are 100 percent silk and handcrafted. If it's cheap, it probably isn't.

Like ethnic crafts, hilltribe motifs and natural materials? Check out Villagecraft Planet, east of the market at 37 Phan Boi Chau Street. Here you can find clothes, bags, cushion covers and other decorative items made from Hmong textiles, batik indigo, hemp and natural dyes.

It'll be hard to resist purchasing one of Hoi An's signature silk lanterns. Stroll the town at night or browse the night market across the river on An Hoi

Islet and the colourful glow will tug at your heart strings. You can buy a few, or try making your own at a workshop offered by Lifestart Foundation, a not-for-profit charity that offers vocational training and assistance to the disadvantaged. The one and a half hour workshop, held at either 10:30-12:00 or 15:30-17:00, costs 330,000 dong per person, with a minimum of two people required to run it. It's the same price for their Vietnamese painting class (09:00-1:30/14:00-15:30). Register in advance. At their shop you can also buy handmade jewellery, fantastic natural body products, loveable stuffed animals made from socks, cards, tea, Co Tu ethnic handicraft, prints, scarves.

Tailoring

Hoi An has become synonymous with tailoring and it seems every other shop in the UNESCO old town is devoted to selling you new custom duds. The tailoring process can be overwhelming. Where does one begin? Here's our guide to tailoring in Hoi An.

Flashback to 2009: Hoi An's reputation as a tailoring mecca was already flourishing and eye-catching samples of pretty frocks adorned storefronts. We wanted to make a dress. We did our research, went to the best, most reputable tailor shop in town armed with a photo, picked out the fabric and plunked down more money than a week's worth of accommodation in Vietnam. It would be worth it, we told ourselves. The first fitting wasn't quite right but it was fairly close to what we wanted. The second fitting was a regression it actually looked worse and something was very off. At the third fitting, the staff assigned to us was anxious to get it done. Suddenly the salesperson who had been so sweet and eager when we started became bored, then argumentative and pushy, and with her help we reluctantly became convinced the dress was okay. We carried the dress around in our backpack for months and when we returned home, we never wore it.

We're older and wiser and now understand that a lot can go wrong with getting clothes made in Hoi An. The first question you should ask is "How much do I care if it's not perfect?" If you just want a button down shirt and not an exact replica of a hot off the runway outfit, then practically any shop will do. But if you are more particular, read on.

The scoop Would it surprise you to know that those "tailor shops" aren't really tailor shops? With very few exceptions, the store you order from isn't doing the actual tailoring. Anyone can set up a shop. It's as easy as buying bolts of fabric, displaying samples on mannequins, buying measuring tape. The sewing is outsourced to "workshops" (the polite word for sweatshops) or seamstresses at the market.

General activities

Cam Kim and other islands

If you limit yourself to Hoi An's historic town and the beach, you're missing out. The town's Thu Bon River has a vast network of islands and islets perfect for two-wheel exploration. Until recently, Cam Kim Island was only connected to the mainland by ferry. But a new bridge makes it even easier to explore. Cycle down quiet roads, past lush paddies and waterways fringed with water coconut palms.

Many Hoi An bicycle tours take you to the various islands and show you the best spots but for a less formal approach, hire your own wheels and go for an exploratory cruise.

To get to Cam Kim Island, first cross over to An Hoi Islet, just across the river from town. In the southwest corner of the An Hoi is the Cam Kim bridge. It doesn't take long to be swept over by a sense of rural calm as the sound of motorbikes disappears, and the most activity comes in the form of fishermen on wooden canoes casting nets into the water.

Once you cross the bridge, you have many options. Turn right and head west along the river until you see signs for Thuy Ta Song Quefollow them through a labyrinth of lanes that end up at a house peacefully situated at the terminus of an inland waterway. They've built a wooden dining hut overlooking the water and it's a pleasant spot to have a drink. You could easily waste hours here relaxing there's a boat with life jackets that they let guests use for free. They also serve food and we enjoyed a snack of cucumbers fresh from their garden. If you're in a group, why not organise a lunch feast? No English is spoken, so have a Vietnamese speaker call them in advance to prepare a farm fresh chicken: T: (0935) 350 959; (0934) 994 949.

South of this spot, in the northwest corner of the island, is Triem Tay village, first settled at the start of the 17th century and home to around 150 families. Clearly an attempt was made to set up the village for tourists there are signs at every corner pointing you to sights of interest, there are maps and info placards throughout

Hoi An for families

Offering both cultural activities and great beaches, Hoi An is a deservedly popular choice for family vacations. There's plenty to keep everyone busy, fed and entertained.

What to do Of all the beaches around Hoi An, An Bang is the easiest with kids. It's just a five-minute, US$5 taxi ride from town and there are a slew of family friendly restaurants to choose from. Most are designed to be hang out spots and for the price of a meal, guests can use the shaded loungers, sun huts, toilets, showers and the grassy area for the little ones to run around.

An Bang is ideal from March to October. During the hottest months, An Bang boasts shallow waters and few or no waves. A few shops sell beach toys and there's plenty available to borrow or hire, including boogie boards, balls and buckets. In addition to Western and Vietnamese beach fare, Soul Kitchen has a pool table, board games, books and some shady nooks perfect for a little nap. It's all very laidback. Soul Kitchen's neighbours are also decent spots to settle in for R&R. Kids and teens will dig the pizza at Luna D'Autonno.

Teens might also take to SUP. If they can be roused at the crack of dawn, the Aloha Tour (US$50) by SUP Monkey is in the shallows of the coastal stretch from Ha My down to An Bang beach where the sea is most calm

Food tours

Food tours are a way to explore Hoi An through the lens of all things delicious. Here are some of the offerings.

We previously reviewed chirpy, cheeky Phuoc and his Coconut Tours street food crawl, and we were pleased as punch with the experience. Phuoc started up his street food tours in earnest after the little thatched cooking school he'd set up in his grandmother's garden blew down in a 2013 typhoon.

The tour begins away from the tourist epicentre of the old town on a street sprawling and vibrant, where dozens of stalls groan under the weight of brightly coloured produce, steaming vats of soup and family-recipe delicacies, all peeking out behind a mad motorbike take-away scene. Get a crash course on everything from condiments to com ga, visiting stalls that Phuoc has been eating at for almost three decades. His introductions, storytelling and running commentary adds a richness to the food itself. And with the food, be as tame or adventurous as you desire perhaps that desire will include trung vit lon (duck fetus egg) or duck congee served with a plate of brain, blood cake and offal. You can now find his tours under Eat Hoi An. The street food tour kicks off at 14:00 and costs US$40.

Hoi An Food Safari guides guests through the jungle of morning street food (US$50 per person). This foot tour starts at 07:30, ends at noon with a whole lot of tasting in between. The goal is a minimum of 15 different eats.

The plainly named Hoi An Food Tour also does a morning street food walking tour. First wake up a Vietnamese coffee before hitting up spots for bites like white rose dumplings, black sesame sweet soup and fried wontons, US$39.

Finally, with The Last Great Taste of Hoi An, Australian Neville Dean enthusiastically takes guests on a whirlwind journey to all his favourite haunts. This is a great option if time is not on your side..

Day trips

Lang Co

Many daytrip destinations from Hoi An can be done with a run-of-the-mill guided tour that tick off a laundry list of tourist sights. For an independent adventure that is cheap, filled with local colour (and flavours) and remains relatively unexplored, check out the area around Lang Co.

Lang Co is a small town on the other side of the Hai Van Pass from Da Nang. Its existence hinges on three things. It's a throughway, with major Highway 1A zipping right through town. Fishing: it's sandwiched between the coast and an enormous seawater lagoon that's stocked with shellfish farms growing mussels, oysters and clams. And it has miles and miles of coast; during the hot, dry months from around March until October, this is a great place to check out some very low-key beaches. The town itself is rather unattractive and not worth spending time in except to have a seafood meal at one of the restaurants perched on the lagoon.

There are three ways to reach Lang Co from Da Nang: Go up 496 metres and over the scenic Hai Van Pass, a route that was thrust into the limelight by an episode of BBC TV show Top Gear. The most popular way for travellers is to rent a motorbike or take an Easy Rider-type motorcycle tour. Cycling diehards can tackle the route solo or with a bicycle tour company, but be warned, it is a strenuous challenge! The second option is to go via the Hai Van Tunnel, which opened in 2005.

At 6.2 kilometres, it is the longest tunnel in Southeast Asia. A small toll fee applies. Motorbikes are not allowed to drive through so you'd have to take a passenger/bike shuttle; this is the best option at night or if the weather is miserable, as the pass can be dangerous in stormy or foggy

Cham Island

Eight nautical miles off the coast of Hoi An, a cluster of eight islands known as Cham Island, or Cu Lao Cham, offers travellers a little getaway. The main island Hon Lao, the largest and the only one inhabited, is less than two hours' away by public boat or a harrowing zip across by speed boat. It boasts beaches, diving, snorkelling, seafood and one very scenic drive. If you're impressed with Hoi An's An Bang Beach, wait until you see Cham's white sand and sparkling turquoise waters.

Most tourists who visit do so on an organised day tour. It is possible to stay overnight on the island and even camp out in a tent on the beach. But the island does just about everything to discourage backpackers from striking out on their own, while encouraging mass group tours. Talk about environmental impact: on the weekends, this means over a thousand people arrive to the beach like they're waging an invasion.

There are several challenge for independent travellers. Foreigners are not allowed to ride motorbikes on the island; the reason we were given is that the roads are too dangerous (indeed, they are extremely steep) but more likely it's because the island is also a military outpost and the government is forever worried about prying eyes as a spat with China over water territory continues to simmer. Without motorbike or bicycle rentals, it's very difficult to get around from beach to beach. Then there's the ridiculous admission fee for the beach and the matter of foreigners getting ripped off on the chaotic public boat. So is a trip to Cham Island worth it?

If you're a beach bum, then yes, though don't expect a deserted idyll. And you'll want to stay overnight so once the swarm of daytrippers and speed boats all depart in the mid-afternoon, you can enjoy the surf and sand in relative peace

My Son

Quang Nam's efforts to market My Son sanctuary as the "Angkor of Vietnam" are a little misguided, but that's not to say it isn't well worth seeing. Those who make the trip expecting to see a vast well-preserved city on par with the incomparable Angkor Wat will be disappointed. However, as the religious and political capital of the Champa Kingdom, it is one of the most significant Cham sites in Vietnam.

Drawing spiritually from Hinduism, the Cham built temples to honour Hindu divinities with fired brick, stone pillars and sandstone bas-reliefs. My Son was initially constructed in the late 4th century, built by King Bhadravarman for the god Shiva (the creator, destroyer and preserver). From then on the temples were continuously developed until the 13th century.

My Son sanctuary became known to the western world in 1885, when French architect, archaeologist and art historian Henri Parmentier (1870-1949) and his colleagues began excavating and documenting the site. They found 72 monuments within a semi-circular, two-kilometre wide valley. Though what you see today are groups of towers simply dotted throughout the forest, the construction of a temple was based on precise holy ritual and imbued with meaning.

A good guide or a visit to the on-site museum is highly recommended before you scamper about the ruins. The museum will help you identify and understand the Hindu symbolism and mythology shown in the architectural designs and motifs. One of the most important representations that you will see in Champa culture is the god Shiva, visible in both anthropomorphic (human) form and symbolically as a linga, a cylindrical block (male, phallus), usually paired with yoni, representing the goddess Shakti (female, womb).

The Ho Chi Minh Trail with Hoi An Motorbike Adventures

With almost 1,000 miles of remote backwater paths and trails, paddy, narrow mountain passes, isolated hill tribes and dense jungle, Vietnam's Ho Chi Minh Trail is one of the most rewarding and directionally challenging rides in the country. Unless you have a penchant for getting lost somewhere near the Lao border or breaking down on the outskirts of heavily guarded forestry land sites you'll want to take a guide and quite possibly a mechanic along for the ride. We saddled up with Hoi An Motorbike Adventures; their deal sealer was a squadron of Belorussian Minsks, also known as "Old Buffalo" by the locals — something about them being reliable old workhorses.

Personally, I'm a bit of a liability on a bike with over 49cc's and although there is a part of me that would just love to have strapped on my helmet and barrelled down the steep, narrow zig-zagging mountain trails, I chose the backseat driving position. A good tip for the non-rider would be to travel with the guide where you get pole position for all the things worth seeing and the rider gets to rip it up a bit without fear of taking you down with them.

We took a two-day tour from Hoi An with an overnight in Ba Hom, an isolated hilltribe village inaccessible by car and inhabited by the Ca Tu, a former headhunting community of incredibly colourful villagers who speak an ancient dialect of Vietnamese. The steady ride there through paddy and tea plantations, bypassing busy A roads and thundering lorries, was breathtaking. We wove along rewarding single track roads flanked by lush steamy jungle and tiny villages oozing with culture and colour.

The feeling of riding up a steep mountain and hitting the rapid temperature drop of low hanging mountain clouds before turning a corner to a peak basked in sunshine, where the vast landscape of rural Vietnam stretches as far as the eye can see, is one of those priceless moments I'd never tire of.

And just as the symptoms of lack of blood flow to my extremities began to set in we arrived at the king of the Ca Tu tribe's abode, where we were welcomed with green tea and invited to check out his extraordinarily detailed wood carving project (his coffin). He then sent us off to our stilted village with a twilight tipple of rice wine.

Ba Hom village has been a project in the making for several years. It's home to a small population of Ca Tu families, and arriving there feels like taking a huge step back in time, both due to its remote location and the fact that it has somehow managed to sidestep the tourist trail. The women wear black and red hand-woven costumes as they have for generations and the men spend their days hunting. Accommodation is basic, but plans are afoot for new-year renovations in a sustainable government project. I however am a fan of basic and after a jungle-scavenged feast prepared by the villagers, I could quite happily have slept on the makeshift football pitch.

Day two of the tour is the Ho Chi Minh Trail, used by the Vietcong to deliver weapons and supplies to the communist guerrillas in the south fighting against both the Southern Vietnamese and American forces during the Vietnam War. Even with the intense bombing the route suffered during the height of the war more than 40 years ago, little has changed and many of the trails are still being used today, fortunately to meet the basic living needs of remote villages rather than weaponry caravans. From the size of the spider that met us at a waterfall hidden down one of the trails, you can't but be in awe of the Vietnamese or fail to understand why the Americans didn't do quite so well roughing it in the jungle.

Usually I'm all for ditching the tour companies and venturing into the unknown with a good map and the spirit of adventure, but without the guys from Hoi An Motorbike Adventures we'd probably still be lost in the jungle somewhere near the Lao border. Having done a similar route with a Nha Trang-based Easy Rider on tiny

Chinese fake Honda Wins, where we negotiated badly and paid $110 per day plus, plus, plus… this was actually quite reasonable, costing us about the same all in at US$185 per day for our more memorable mountain ride on the old buffalos.

Hoi An Motorbike Adventures
111 Ba Trieu St, Hoi An
T: (84) 05103 911930

Yoga

Hoi An offers several styles of yoga classes, from the relaxed to Eka Hasta Vrksasana.

Here's a round up of what's available.

With the longstanding Hoi An Yoga now closed, Nomad Yoga is currently Hoi An's go-to studio. They offer Ashtanga, hatha, gentle classes as well as kids' yoga and meditation. A single drop-in class is 130,000 dong. Check their website for up-to-date pricing and the week's schedule. The studio is located on Le Hong

Phong Street, mid-way between An Bang Beach and town.

Wellness and spa-centric resort Almanity allows outside guests to attend their daily morning yoga class from 07:00 to 08:30, enjoyed in the air-conditioned loveliness of their second floor yoga room. The price is part of a "membership" deal that allows you access to their fitness centre, swimming pool and 20 per cent discounts on spa, food and beverage. The price for one day is 175,000 dong, or 950,000 dong for one month.

Further afield, there are more options in Da Nang. The Maia Spa at Fusion Suites offers class daily, with hatha, yin and vinyasa on offer at a drop-in rate of 220,000 dong. Book in advance. And for something a little more daring, check out Aro Yoga Danang, which offers both traditional yoga and "air" or anti-gravity yoga, which uses a silk hammock (think Cirque-du-Soleil). We haven't tried it but we'd love to see what a flying downward dog looks like. Their pricing is geared towards residents of Da Nang who can buy memberships but for those just dropping in, the price is 500,000 dong per session.

Aro Yoga Danang: 52 Tran Cao Van St, Tam Thuan Ward, Thanh Khe District, Da Nang;
T: (0511) 352 2200; aroyogadanang@gmail.com;

Festivals and events

Full moon lantern festival

If you happen to be in Hoi An on the 14th day of any lunar month, you'll be treated to central Vietnam's version of a full moon party.

The Hoi An lantern festival is an age-old tradition that sees the entire old town shut off electricity, close to traffic and transform into a magical melange of flickering candles, multi-coloured lanterns and lively gatherings.

For the locals the night of the full moon is the time to honour their ancestors by setting up altars and offering fruit and flowers, burning incense and fake money outside homes and businesses in exchange for good luck and prosperity. This is a great time for a temple visit each of the town's pagodas are awash with activities, all free of charge. Monks hold candlelit ceremonies and the Phuc Kien (Fujian) Assembly Hall on Tran Phu Street hosts an inspiring gathering of local fishing families honouring Lady Thien Hau, goddess of the sea. All attractions are free for visitors on the night of the full moon. Other entertainment includes local street musicians playing traditional instruments, poetry readings, Chinese chess matches by candlelight and other traditional theatrics and games such as bai choi, a bit like musical bingo. To have any chance of knowing what on earth is going on, you'll need a guide.

Once you've fought your way past the romantic Vietnamese couples holding hands and photo-bombed quite a few selfies, jostle your way to the riverfront where you'll be accosted by locals selling cardboard lotus flower-shaped lanterns with a candle to be released on the river. We're a bit skeptical about how traditional this actually is but the seller will convince you it will bring happiness, luck and love, all for the low, low price of 10,000 dong like with everything in Vietnam, settle on the price before you release the lantern bearing your wish for future happiness. Those floating lanterns are a beautiful sight but at the risk of being a wet blanket,

Mid-Autumn Festival

The Mid-Autumn Festival, also known as the harvest or children's festival, takes place on the 14th and 15th day of the eighth lunar month, usually falling in September. Marking the end of the final rice harvest of the year, this centuries-old festival is a chance for families to celebrate a good yield, spend time with their children, chase away bad spirits and honour the moon. If we were to choose just one must-see event in Hoi An, this is it.

Hanoi and Saigon may be steaming ahead when it comes to modern development, but rural Vietnam and in particular Hoi An has kept a firmly rooted in tradition as generations of families still hold faith in myths, legends, fables and folklore. For thousands of years these traditions have formed the heart of the community, protecting health, the home and most importantly the family. Hoi An is a great place to experience this festival.

In the weeks leading up to it, the atmosphere in the town and surrounding villages becomes fuelled with excitement as children rehearse their dragon dance and drumming in the street and shops burst with vibrant, elaborate costumes and masks. Friends and family gift each other with boxes of moon cake, a sweet treat filled with a paste made of beans or lotus seeds, often with an egg yolk in the middle. There's salty, savoury versions as well. On the big night, a procession of excited children carry star, moon and animal shaped paper lanterns, which represent the sun circling the moon. Then it's the turn of the dragon dancers to arrive and where the dragons go, the crowd follows. The cheeky dragon visits each shop, business and house to bestow good luck and fortune. They perform a choreographed dance, where the dragon, urged on by a smiley moon faced 'tamer' representing the Lord Earth, enters each building and does its good luck cha-cha-cha. The host then gives lucky money as thanks. It's a riotous affair.

For epic performances, head towards the big businesses in town like Yaly or Cargo as night falls and you will be rewarded with professional dragon dancing teams climbing huge bamboo poles and breathing fire; it's a must-see performance that escapes every health and safety law you can think of and attracts huge crowds. Hold on to your handbag!

Aided by the thousands of paper lanterns on the river, Bach Dang Street is possibly the best-lit spot and from here you can escape on a riverboat tour or work your way to the quieter edge of town, where you will find dozens of kids doing their own dragon performance tour for fun. It feels more authentic and makes for photo opportunities and involvement. Kids go to homes and businesses and ask for permission to perform. Afterwards they will be awarded with lucky money. Give these kids 20,000 dong and you will get your own performance and their parents will love you for it.

Riverside Bach Dang Street, which due to a wider road tends to be the easiest to navigate, is a good meeting point if you get lost amid the madness. Aided by the thousands of paper lanterns on the river, it's possibly the best-lit spot; or work your way to the quieter edge of town, where you will find dozens of kids playing at their own dragon performance for fun, which somehow feels a bit more authentic.

Cooking classes

What gives papaya salad that zing? Where is the best cao lau in town? How do you order Vietnamese coffee like a local? If these are the kinds of burning questions you have (or you just love to eat), Hoi An is a mecca for cooking classes and food tours and just like banh mi stalls, there are plenty to choose from.

There are dozens upon dozens of cooking classes available in Hoi An and which one you should choose simply depends on preference. Some are held in restaurants in town, with an abridged crash course that take as little as an hour, while others are drawn out into day-long affairs combined with a motorbiking, cycling or boating to fishing villages and herb gardens. Do you want a class in town or a rural setting? A restaurant or a home? Does it include a fresh market tour? Do you prefer demonstration style or really getting hands-on, doing all the prep yourself? Want to learn the popular dishes or something that requires a more adventurous palate and dexterous culinary skills? One thing is for sure: you won't leave hungry.

Several of the strongest cooking classes are attached to popular restaurants. The Ms Vy empire of eateries has the cooking class down to an art and there are programs at Vy's Market Restaurant & Cooking School and her longstanding Morning Glory Restaurant. While we like to highlight small enterprises, we also can't deny that this establishment is a solid choice and an organised, well-oiled machine. In addition to your standard class (two hours, four dishes, 550,000 dong), we like that there are also advanced programmes for more serious students. The "Advanced Masterclass" will appeal to at-home-chefs who aren't afraid to get hands-on and put their knife skills to good use. This half-day class (08:30-13:30) includes buying the ingredients at the market and a tour through some street food kitchens.

Cultural areas

Thanh Ha Pottery Village

If you're out exploring Hoi An under your own steam, Thanh Ha pottery village is a decent stop, especially since it's on the way to My Son.

The big landmark is the Terracotta Village, a park and centre devoted to all things pottery. In true

Vietnamese tourism fashion, it is extremely kitsch, with the front garden full of clay replicas of the architectural wonders of the world, everything from the Taj Mahal to the Colosseum in Rome. Why travel the world when you can see it all here!

We actually suggest giving this place a skip. The only other reason you'd want to pay the 30,000 dong admission to this tourist trap is to go play with clay. You can paint a piece of pottery for 50,000 dong, or make your own pottery for 30,000 dong. This may be a good activity to kill an hour with the kids. When we visited, there was a large school group of youngsters that seemed to delight in mucking around with the clay. Despite people trying to lure you to pay to park your motorbike, you can park inside the gate for free.

It's better to head straight to the narrow lanes behind the village tourist park to find the families busy churning out pots, sculptures, roof tiles and cute handcrafted whistles shaped like animals. The potters are welcoming and friendly, and they are happy to offer a seat to watch as they work.

At the workshop with the sign "Chu Ho Le Van Xe"️, we watched as one woman stood and kneaded a huge lump of clay, all while kicking the wheel-head with her foot as another woman worked throwing the pot. (Note: "throwing" is the lingo for forming pottery on the wheel-head. And if you don't know what a wheel-head is, it's a good reason to come here to find out.) It was mesmerising to watch the two steadily churn out perfectly formed pots, and they even offered to let us try.

The new creations are dried in the sun and then fired in a wood-fire kiln

Where to stay in Hoi An

In this town it's a challenge for backpackers and flashpackers to find a hostel that ticks all the boxes: location, cleanliness, friendly staff and atmosphere. One that manages to balance all of these is Phong Le Villa Hostel. Located on An Hoi Islet, it's an easy cycle along the river to the old town while providing guests a laidback pocket to hangout, chill out and socialise. The air-conditioned dorms have beds, not bunks, and those with five beds have oodles of space. The price is on par with other Hoi An hostels, but Phong Le Villa stands out as being backpacker friendly and good value.

If you don't mind the out of the way location, Paddy's Hostel offers backpackers a ton of flashy extras and very comfortable air-con dorms that were refurbished in 2016 (some even sport double beds). It's a friendly, easygoing place and you'll no doubt find yourself relaxing in their ground floor Irish pub, shooting pool or lounging on a sunbed next to the large swimming pool, a luxurious touch for budget travellers. You'll need to rely on bicycles or motorbikes to get around though, as Paddy's is located close to Cua Dai Beach, or three kilometres from the old town. It's worth the distance if you have your heart set on a clean, affordable bed.

Can you believe, Hoi An's prime beach An Bang has accommodation mere steps from the sand for under US$10? The longstanding Under the Coconut Tree Homestay boasts character and is a budget beach bum's dream. Built of bamboo, thatch and rattan, the large dorm house is rustic yet solidly built and well-cared for. Sturdy wood bunks are kitted with mosquito nets, lockers and power outlets, and the bunks are quite spread out to keep everything feeling spacious. It's simple yet has everything a low-key backpacker needs to be close to the beach.

Flashpackers will have to stretch their budgets and spend more than US$20, but at this price you usually do get more bang for your dong (oh dear, that didn't sound right). Let's just say that for US$27, guests are spoiled with clean, comfy, cute rooms at homey Orchids Homestay. The location is ideal (at the eastern edge of the historic centre, in the French Quarter), the owners are friendly and eager to help yet not pushy and the rate includes a hearty breakfast and bicycle rental. A lot of care has been put into the details and maintenance of the incredibly tidy rooms which have air-con, piping hot water, good water pressure and daily housekeeping. You'll look forward to returning at the end of a long day.

Another hotel in the US$20-30 range that gets top marks for fantastic service is Hoang Trinh Hotel. Rooms are old fashioned and orderly, the location is convenient — easy walking distance to the historic centre — and as indicated by the impressive towel art adorning the beds, staff here go the extra mile to please.

Stepping into the mid-range, a cosy book-nook awaits at Vinh Hung Library Hotel. A standout on backpacker block Ba Trieu Street, the library-themed hotel is a bit kitschy though we appreciate their effort to be unique compared to so many of the bland hotels in town. We recommend paying more for the beautifully designed and decorated deluxe rooms that feature natural wood furniture and a sliding glass door leading to a balcony shrouded in greenery. The rooftop plunge pool is a bonus.

At the mid-range level, we start looking closely at value for money and it's clear that going outside of the town centre will yield better value. Rock Villa is a perfect example. Sandwiched between a river and rice paddy, not only are the rooms stylish, there's a welcoming swimming pool and plenty of space to spread out. Chill out in the garden, by the river, your balcony or under the communal covered terrace. The family who run this place is lovely to boot.

You may choose Red Flower Cottage Homestay for its fantastic location on An Bang Beach but you'll remember your stay for Ms Kim, who goes out of her way to ensure her guests are happy and in want of nothing. It's homey hospitality that could outshine a five-star hotel, a perfect compliment to these low-key, breezy modern cottages at US$45 a night.

If you have more to spend, you're really spoiled for choice in Hoi An. A boutique hotel with the works can be had for US$50-100. For less than US$70, enjoy exceptional service at Hoi An Ancient House Village Resort and Spa. Surrounded by countryside and endowed with lush tropical gardens, the 56-room property doesn't feel overly big or impersonal. Rooms have all the high-end hotel creature comforts and the restaurant and pool overlook a serene rice paddy. The free shuttle will whisk guests to town or An Bang Beach, alleviating any qualms about being three kilometres from town.

If a location in town is important, Lantana Boutique is one of our top picks. It ticks the boxes: riverside location, steps to the historic quarters, chic decor, restful rooms with river views. The US$50 room rate is an absolute steal and it includes buffet breakfast, underground swimming pool, decent gym and shuttle to An Bang with their own chairs set up for guests.

Finally, splurge and splash at Almanity, a wellness-centric oasis that offers a resort atmosphere with a location close to the old town. The hotel wraps around an inviting, generously sized courtyard pool. It also boasts a spa — the room rate includes one spa treatment and yoga classes. The rooms themselves are in line with the spa theme: calm, cool and chic. Look for online deals, as we noticed good discounts off the regular rack rate.

Hoi An old town

Most guesthouses and hotels in Hoi An are within easy walking distance of the historic old quarter but relatively few are within its immediate confines. Those that are tend to be overpriced.

Hoi An has excellent options for mid-range and top-range budgets -- you can get a hotel with the works for

US$50-100 -- but backpackers and flashpackers will struggle. Decent dorms cost around US$10 and will be a good 10-minute walk from the town; flashpackers will need to spend more than US$20 to get an acceptable level of cleanliness and comfort, but you do usually get bicycle and breakfast included.

The town is enormously popular, with too many package tours, and prices reflect this. The lines between the traditional high season and low season have blurred and prices fluctuate at any time with demand. That said, with so much competition and more hotels opening, we noticed deep discounts off rack rates online. If you walk into a small family-run guesthouse, you may be able to bargain a little. Any more formal establishment and the opposite is true. The staff don't have the authority to give discounts and will quote you the rack rate, when you can simply go online and book it for up to 50% off. So frugal travellers, it is definitely worth doing some comparison shopping.

Almanity

A two-storey hotel that wraps around a large courtyard pool, this wellness-centric resort and spa is an oasis close to Hoi An old town.

The multi-tiered pool is the property's best feature. Surrounded by palms, sun beds, tables and umbrellas, it's large enough so everyone can spread out. At the far end, stairs sweep up to the spa, the hotel's second selling point; the room rate includes one spa treatment. The lofty spa lobby is a serene space, and offerings include manicures and pedicures, massages, sauna and complimentary yoga.

The rooms themselves are calm and comfortable, decorated in neutral and soft hues, clean contemporary lines and elegant furnishings. Patterned tiles and antique style fixtures add some personality, as does the balcony. Rooms include a minibar, very comfortable bed, flatscreen TV, WiFi, safety box, kettle and bathroom amenities. All guests can look forward to a generous breakfast buffet spread.

Almanity is for those with a little more to spend. It is fantastic value if you get a deal off the rack rate. We noticed significant discounts on online booking sites compared to the regular rate. It is located northwest of the old town, about a 15-minute walk or a quick taxi ride away.

Orchids Homestay

Orchids Homestay is perfectly situated for someone who wants to be close to the old town and river.

Located at the eastern edge of the historic centre, in the French quarter a couple blocks east of the market and diagonally across from Anantara Resort, this guesthouse has just six affordable rooms, the deal sweetened by the free bicycle rental, air-con and WiFi, as well as a hearty breakfast -- eggs, noodle soup, fresh fruit -- ordered the night before.

The immaculately tidy rooms have a touch more charm and functionality than your average Vietnamese hotel:

parquet wood floors, a handy clothing-luggage rack, wooden desk/vanity, bedside table and lamp, and a comfortable bed strewn with frangipanis upon arrival. Travellers can enjoy the flatscreen TV and a bathroom with a separate shower stall and piping hot water with good pressure. There's hot water for the sink as well. The fridge is loaded up with a few minibar drinks and there's daily housekeeping with fresh towels to boot.

Some rooms are better than others. The two family rooms (either four twins beds or two double beds) are large and have a balcony. Others have a frosted window out to the hall --better than not having any window at all but you don't get true sunlight. The only other downside is you can hear the noisy comings and goings of other guests in the hallways.

Orchids is an easy stroll to the walking street. This area is very quiet after 20:00, so it's good for bed rest but for those walking solo, it is a bit eerily dark. The owners speak great English and they respond to emails lightning fast. Note: the Vietnamese word for orchid -- hoa phong lan is on the front sign.

Anantara Hoi An Resort

Anantara Hoi An (formerly the Life Resort) is a spacious property on the Thu Bon River at the eastern edge of Hoi An old town.

The French colonial-style buildings are set in an immaculate tropical garden which has plenty of space to roam and a modestly sized swimming pool.

While the exteriors are charming, the resort has the challenges a reputable company faces when taking over an existing property -- the rooms aren't of the best design. Most of the 93 rooms have the same basic layout, though the deluxe suites are slightly larger. Connected by an open corridor, each room has a front porch with sitting area. Inside, the bed is awkwardly sandwiched between a living space and the bathroom door. The bathroom, though modern and obviously recently upgraded, has issues as the shower has no curtain or door and water sprays everywhere.

It seens they've done touch ups, though when we stayed in a Junior Garden View Suite in 2015, the uncomfortable mattress, thin pillows and clunky, loud air-con directly over the bed needed to be replaced. This hotel is hopefully a work in progress.

The original structure of the building presents design challenges but the exceptionally pretty property, the location (an easy bike ride or stroll to town), service and experience of staying on the river overshadows the flaws. What you can expect are all the four-star amenities and excellent service. Rooms come with air-con, WiFi, safety box, minibar, a plate of fruit, posh toiletries, hair dryer and evening turn down. There's a spa, a generous breakfast buffet spread in their restaurant overlooking the river, two bars, weekly buffet dinners and a trip on their private boat.

Cozy Hoian Villas

While there is nothing actually "villa" about it (there are 17 rooms), the rooms are pleasant in its modern design and decor. Plush bed, vanity, flatscreen TV, minibar, WiFi, air-con and balcony are standard to all rooms. Rooms have been jazzed up with floor tiles adorned with patterns, bright cushions, playful lanterns and a small but swish bathroom with tiled shower and a rain showerhead.

They've even managed to squeeze in a small triangular shaped pool, suitable for a cool off and with a few stylish loungers to hang out on. The room rate includes breakfast and bicycle, which you'll want to take advantage of because it is a kilometre's walk along the river to town. Cozy Hoian Villas is tucked down a local lane that runs north off the river road (Nguyen Du). The low season rates are very reasonable for what you get.

La Residencia

The immediate surrounds are sterile and even though it's on the river, it is not an interesting part of it. However, it is a short walk to the old town and being a more recent build, the hotel has perks like an enormous basement lap pool, well-equipped gym and a pleasant bar/dining area.

The rooms themselves are pretty, a mix of old world and new. The patterned floor tile, patina copper bathroom fixtures, French balcony and world furniture have old-timey flair, while bold wall colours, enormous flatscreen TV, lovely bed and air-con deliver contemporary comfort. Amenities include kettle, WiFi, minibar, fresh fruit, safety box, desk, cosmetic mirror, a bathroom with a spacious shower stall and toiletries. The high categories have more space, as well as a vantage over the river though we don't think you should upgrade unless you really have your heart set on it.

Are those pretty tiles and costume-y fixtures durable? Only time will tell. For now, the room rate, the decent breakfast spread with both Western and Vietnamese fare, and proximity to the historic town does make this a solid choice for those with more to spend. If you're shopping around, check out comparable Lantana just across the river.

Strawberry Garden Homestay

There needs to be a good reason for us to recommend an accommodation 1.5 kilometres east of the old town, and we found several at this tranquil homestay of four rooms.

The gated property is located down a quiet local lane. The garden has tables and chairs to relax in if you get bored of your private balcony/terrace -- each room has one. The house is new and modern and the rooms reflect that. They are clean, spacious and equipped with modern comforts: air-con, WiFi, flatscreen TV, a breakfast table set, large windows with security bars, minifridge, a wardrobe with mirror and a sparkling new large bathroom with both a bathtub and shower. There's no separate shower stall -- it's a wetroom bathroom -- but you do get a handy inbuilt nook to place all the toiletries. It's a room you could easily feel comfortable staying in for a while.

You'll definitely want to take advantage of the free bicycle to get into town, an easy, flat 10-minute ride following the river. Breakfast is included. This place will appeal to those who want some peace and greenery.

Thien Nga Hotel

It provides far more modernity and comfort than other similarly priced hotels in the area, and the view from the balcony in the superior rooms are a big selling point.

On a previous review of this property, it had been recently renovated. As of May 2016, cheerful pale yellow walls look like they could use a fresh coat of paint and the beds, which feel like a foam mattress, could use new linens. However, the bones of the room are great as you get solid wood desk, wardrobe with a full length mirror, flatscreen TV, minibar, bedside plugs, safety box, air-con and WiFi. Fixtures and the bathtub/shower combo in the bathroom feel dated, though you can't fault the clean tiles and bright lighting.

Balconies have a patio set, and it's the spot to grab a minute of relaxation after a day haggling with Hoi An's tailors. If you can, get a room in the back for a view over the neighbouring crops. You can also relax on a terrace at the front of the hotel or out back, next to the small undercover pool. At this rate, the rooms are good value and within reach for flashpackers. It's a standout on Ba Trieu Street, which has plenty of backpacker hovels.

Vinh Hung 1 Heritage Hotel

Vinh Hung 1 Heritage Hotel is one of them. Located smack dab in the heart of the pedestrian zone, this hotel gives guests a chance to live a bit of history.

You might recognise this beautiful wooden Chinese trading house from the iconic film-based-on-novel The Quiet American, starring Michael Caine (Suite 208 served as the star's dressing room during filming). Walk past it on Tran Phu and you may assume it's one of the sights on your UNESCO ticket. We were told the building is 200 years old, and after being bought from a Chinese merchant in 1992, it was one of the very first hotels to open its doors to tourism. Step into the atmospheric reception, full of dark lacquer furniture and antiques, and it's like stepping back in time.

Though it has gone through a few renovations, its most recent upgrade has lifted it into a creaky but classy six-room hotel that oozes mystery and old world charm.

There are six rooms, the Chinese-style balcony suites on the upstairs floor being the best. Imagine being able to sit up there with a glass of chilled wine watching the tourists scurry below. From the small inner sanctum, intriguing shadowy wooden hallways lead to wood rooms furnished with traditional furniture, but are otherwise equipped with modern amenities. These comforts include minibar, air-con, flatscreen TV, safety box, kettle, WiFi and a completely modern bathroom with contemporary fixtures, hair dryer and large bathtub. It won't be perfect -- it's an old building after all -- but it does make for a memorable experience that is incomparable to anything else in Hoi An. You either understand the intangible value or you don't.

The hotel is hauntingly beautiful, though there is the slight air of the ramshackled and unrefined-- the receptionist was abrupt and we noticed odds and ends haphazardly stacked up on chairs in the lobby. You can get a lot more for half the price at any number of resorts just outside the old town. Here you'll get no breakfast buffet, spa, garden, lively service or pool, though you are allowed to use the pool at their sister property Vinh Hung Riverside Resort. If you need to be sold on this property or the room rate, it's probably not for you. This is for those who want a place that tells a story.

Vinh Hung Library Hotel

The 24-room mid-range hotel sits behind a veil of tumbling bougainvillea on popular with backpackers Ba Trieu Street.

Inside, it has a cosy comfort that people associate with their local reading room. The walls of the lobby/breakfast buffet dining area are lined with books and the hallways are full of cheerful pizzazz in the form of colourful art. It's bold and perhaps a bit kitschy, but we're digging the effort to be different.

Despite the fact that they are on the small side, the deluxe rooms feel airy and light, achieved with the tidy white linen spread across the thick mattress, the canopy of mosquito net and sliding glass doors leading out to the balcony shrouded by greenery. There's a sense of gentle refinement in the design details such as natural wood furniture, a large scale decorative piece above the beds, a pop of colour from a few bedside lanterns, photos of river life and display of pottery on the shelves. Don't forget the practical comforts: bedside table and plug, WiFi, air-con, large flatscreen TV and kettle. The only downside to the bathroom is the dim lighting and the prefabricated modular shower stall which large folk will find cramped.

The superior rooms are windowless and dimly lit, though it still has the same cozy-chic design and a built in sofa. But at US$36 per night, it is a hard sell and you won't struggle to find something cheaper for the same calibre. In contrast, we think the deluxe rooms are worth it. All rates include buffet breakfast.

The rooftop pool should be viewed as an added bonus,

not the selling point. The deck has enough room to squeeze in a picnic table and some loungers, there's a change room and the pool itself will satisfy those who want to submerge on a hot day, not do to laps or show off your synchronised swimming routine.

Ha An Hotel

Set around a manicured garden, the two-storey buildings are designed to look like an old Hoi An shop house. Inside though, the interiors are tidy and modern Vietnamese, with tile floor, plain wood furniture and amenities such as flatscreen TV, fridge, kettle, air-con, WiFi and a functional bathroom. The rooms with the terrace facing the garden are very pleasant. The courtyard also has a billiard table and hammocks. Bicycle and breakfast are included.

There's nothing wrong with the room and it is an intimate setting, but it is expensive for what you get. We'd expect it to be more stylish for the price, which we suspect is inflated given its location, its proximity to the river and the heritage feel of the surrounding buildings. If you're comparison shopping for value and the actual rooms, you may want to consider less expensive Lantana on the opposite side of town, though Lantana doesn't have the old town setting.

Hoang Trinh Hotel

Though the room interiors are dated, they do make an effort with service and some amazing towel art.

The days of their US$10-20 rooms are long gone. Hoang Trinh's room rate is a stretch for backpackers but the front-facing rooms and the second-floor breakfast balcony look straight over a magnificent Confucius temple on busy Tran Hung Dao. However, being set back on quiet Le Quy Don lane, you are away from the bustle. Slip down a little alley opposite and you'll come out in the quieter, artsy side of the Japanese Bridge.

Rooms are old-fashioned, solid and tidy. They come

with WiFi, air-con, vanity/desk, sitting area and flatscreen TV. The tile bathroom has a sink with countertop and a bathtub/shower combo.

As for value for money, we do think it is slightly on the high side. For example, bicycles are not provided. Then again, not many other budget hotels have staff lined up waiting to receive you with such a warm reception. The hotel attracts a mixed and slightly older crowd. If you are looking for a party hotel or to save money, then you'll probably head to Ba Trieu Street which has a glut of overpriced but cheaper windowless hotels. The atmosphere at Hoang Trinh is far more guest-oriented, a one-star hotel with four-star staff happy to go the extra mile.

Like Hoi An Hotel

At that time, you can get this midrange hotel at flashpacker prices.

Being on the outskirts does mean you get more for

your money and the hotel helps bridge the one kilometre distance by offering free bicycle rental, as well as frequent shuttles to town and a twice a day shuttle to An Bang Beach. Like Hoi An, which was formerly Thanh Van 2 Hotel, is located on the corner of Hai Ba Trung and Ton Duc Thang streets, north of the old town on the way to An Bang Beach; it's a 15-minute walk or a quick bicycle ride to town. Given its location, it is a larger hotel by Hoi An standards and it also means the 37-rooms are spacious and there's an outdoor ground floor swimming pool.

The upstairs superior rooms won't win style awards yet they are comfortable and come with all the usual wood hotel furnishings laid out on clean tile floors. You get a desk/vanity, full-length mirror, TV, air-con, WiFi, sitting area with hard wooden seats, wardrobe, safety box, bathrobes and a marble bathroom with modern fixtures and a bathtub/shower combo. Deluxe rooms do feel like an upgrade, with wooden floors, a sofa and a small balcony overlooking the town.

Despite being a large local hotel, we found reception to be extremely courteous and enthusiastic. A buffet breakfast is included and the hotel also has a spa. The room rate and design attracts a mixed crowd: flashpackers, both Vietnamese and foreign families and returning guests. It's the kind of place an expat would put up visiting friends and family. It is also surrounded by authentic Vietnamese dining options. Another bonus: the position back from the main road into town means that it tends not to flood.

Thien Thanh Boutique Hotel

A 2012 refurbishment has transformed it into a quaint, charming spot despite the fact it is on Ba Trieu, a road packed with backpacker joints. The 16-rooms come with great service and lovely extras such as a swimming pool and large deck with paddy views. It's not usual to find such greenery so close to the old town. This is the perfect spot to mix town and country, within a 10-minute walk of the historic centre and one of the quietest centrally located hotel we have come across.

There's an instant ambience as you climb the narrow stairs -- like most hotels close to the old town, there are skinny stairwells and no lift. Rooms at the back overlook the morning glory fields, and you can lap up the view from the private balcony. These balcony rooms at the back are worth the extra dong. The interiors are well-appointed and have Vietnamese flair with red and black accents carried throughout. Rooms have a purpose built solid wood desk/vanity/minibar equipped with a kettle, a flatscreen TV, WiFi, air-con and a swish bathroom with modern fixtures, sink with countertop, hair dryer and bathtub with rain showerhead. They've perhaps gone too fancy for their own good, using stepping stones surrounded by pebbles for the flooring.

The standard rooms are small windowless boxes with just the right amount of furniture and correct layout to make it feel uncluttered. It would be ideal for one, cramped for two.

The showstopper is the suite in the eaves, with its exposed Hoi An-style tile ceiling and panoramic views across the city.

The big selling point is the pool and the large deck with loungers and tables. From it you can hear more bird song than motorbike honking. It's a little oasis, and it's priced just right. The rate includes breakfast.

Tribee Hostel

It also has a location in the heart of the backpacker street Ba Trieu, close to the old town.

The air-con dorm rooms are simply converted hotel rooms, which means it fits just three beds (not bunks), has windows and the shared wetroom-style bathroom is ensuite. The mattress looks a bit thin, but each bed gets a plug and there are hooks on the wall for drying your towel (towel not included). An enormous locker lies underneath each, large enough for your backpack and then some. The dorm we saw smelled strongly of feet, but that's just the luck of the draw with your dorm mates because all shoes are left at the front entrance. Routers placed throughout the hallway means there's WiFi for whatever dorm you're in.

The private rooms are less stellar value. They are functional charmless tile boxes with air-con, a bed, bedside table and plug, box TV, a small window and a fridge. Maybe that's all a hardcore backpacker needs in their private room.

The rate includes breakfast and there's a good feeling in the small, colourful lobby with smiley staff. Suggested itineraries are posted on the wall as well as all the usual bus and tour bookings available. Tribee is one of the better hostels in town, a place where there are very few recommendable ones.

Vesper Homestay

Vesper Homestay is located 1.5 kilometres north of the old town, on the way to An Bang. It's a family home with five rooms and the friendly family provides a warm welcome. Flashpackers can look forward to startlingly clean, minimalist modern rooms. The deluxe room is fab: spacious, white walls, large windows you can open and with its own cute, narrow balcony veiled by greenery. It also comes with a vanity/desk, flatscreen TV, fan, comfortable bed, clean linens and large wetroom bathroom with hot water. Superior rooms are on the small side, perfect for one but tight for two.

If cleanliness, comfort or quiet are your main concern, it's worth the eight-minute cycle to town. There's an explosion of accommodation labelled "homestay" in Hoi An these days, but few places really endeavour to make you feel welcome like the family at Vesper. Guests stay in a local lane so this would be an ideal spot for weary travellers looking for a bit of hospitality and quiet location. Party animals look elsewhere.

Vesper is easy to find. Continue north on Phan Dinh Phung until you reach a dead end, which is a block north of Ly Thai To Street. The paved road ends and you turn right down the dirt path. While there has been some new development around it, Vesper gives you a sliver of rural life.

Volar Homestay

Each of the seven rooms has some sort of balcony or terrace, laminate floors, a comfy bed with even comfier linens and a neutral decor of white, brown and beige. Bathrooms are swish by backpacker standards: contemporary fixtures, a separate shower stall with two types of shower heads. Bicycle, breakfast, air-con and WiFi are included. There's also a communal rooftop terrace, though it is in definite need of some shade or greenery.

There's no view of anything and it's in a new development area, so there's not much soul either, but for those looking for a clean, comfortable, modern room at a flashpacker price, Volar Homestay has seven of them. Keep in mind it's about an eight-minute bike ride to town.

An Hoi islet

Located just across the Hoai River from the old town, An Hoi Islet is easily accessible by three bridges, including a popular pedestrian bridge close to the landmark Japanese Bridge. It's a great place to stay to be close to the historic centre and get river views.

Lantana Boutique Hotel

The rooms at Lantana are almost a carbon copy of La Residencia, right down the pattern floor tiles, patina copper fixtures and basement pool/gym. It's so similar that we asked if they were the same owner (apparently not). Opened in 2015, Lantana has a slight edge. It is just a bit spiffier and luxurious, giving guests a feeling that this is even more of a steal.

Lantana is located on the other side of the river, on the northern edge of An Hoi Islet looking back at the mainland. The pseudo French colonial exterior with shades of antebellum is twee, but who cares about the exterior because the rooms are tasteful and elegant, balancing decor with comfort. Enter a room and it feels like a calming exhale. The room we saw had light grey walls, white linens, dark wood furniture, blue quilted throw pillows and bed runner. Watercolour paintings adorned the wall and the bathroom had everything a traveller needed: contemporary fixtures, a blue tiled shower stall with dispensers of soaps and lotions. Lux amenities included large wall mounted flatscreen TV, desk, minibar, safety box, air-con and WiFi. If you can afford it, the deluxe river view room is worth it as you get your own private balcony.

Though they rate themselves a four-star, it's really an excellent three-star. Our only concern is how well everything stands the test of time, whether materials were chosen because they were good quality or because they were pretty. The room rate includes a buffet breakfast, an L-shaped underground swimming pool, well-equipped gym, a three times a day shuttle to An Bang and a "private" section of the beach with chairs. The terrace at the front of the house seals this deal. No bicycles are provided -- it's an easy seven-minute walk to the old town. Head east, cross the pedestrian bridge and you'll be right at the landmark Japanese Bridge.

Phong Le Villa Hostel

Backpackers will feel close enough to the action but also get a slice of Hoi An island life in this pocket.

Compared to some of the lacklustre hostels and dorms we saw, Phong Le has a more civilised approach, where beds (not bunks) aren't crammed in. The four-bed dorm is of a decent size, while the five-bed dorms have oodles of space. We'd actually prefer the latter. Guests get a backpack-sized lockers, air-con as well as fan, ensuite shared bathroom and WiFi, all in a clean modern building. Beds have individual reading lights and electrical outlet. The room rate also includes breakfast and one free drink. Should you need your own space, there are private rooms as well.

Phong Le Villa has set up a great social space to hang out in their front-of-house pavilion that acts as their lobby/bar/chill out area. There's chairs, tables, picnic tables, bean bags, hammocks: clearly they really want you to hangout, which you can do after a tour or before one of their pub crawls.

Phong Le Villa is located on the river, on the north side of An Hoi Islet near the western tip. A taxi will be able to take you directly there, Thoai Ngoc Hau Street is accessible to cars. It's just west of the 18 Thang 8 Street bridge.

An Bang Beach

An Bang, Hoi An's star beach, is five kilometres from town, located up the coast from eroded Cua Dai Beach. Accommodation is currently limited to small homestays and cottages, many just a short walk to the sand. Bigger hotels are on the horizon.

Christina's Hoi An

To get to An Bang, you'll take Hai Ba Trung Road and just before you reach the coast, the road runs right through Tra Que Village, an isle known for its many vegetable gardens and farms. Nestled at the northern edge of this isle and overlooking the river is Christina's Hoi An, a chic boutique hotel with pretty and spacious contemporary rooms.

All rooms have the same layout. What varies is the view -- pool, garden or river, the latter best enjoyed from rooms on the upper levels and especially in the corner one, which has windows on both sides. Interiors are stylish and soft, with white walls, crisp white linens, clean modern lines and dark wood floors complimented with a few pops of bright colours. Air-con, WiFi, flatscreen TV and fluffy towels are standard amenities. The enormous bathroom is divine -- oversized stone sinks, huge countertop, fancy bathtub and shower -- but its open concept will have detractors. A dividing wall separates it from the bedroom and there's no door. Hopefully you're comfortable with your travel partner.

If you get tired of swimming in the ocean, the large lap pool at your doorstep will keep you entertained. The room rate includes breakfast and bicycle, which you'll want to explore the pretty surrounding countryside or to make the 4.5 kilometre cycle into the old town. Beach and quiet greenery, Christina's Hoi An has a foot in each.

Red Flower Cottage Homestay

Situated a hop and a skip to the An Bang Beach and all its bars and restaurants, Red Flower has five comfortable cottages that will please mid-range seekers or flashpackers willing to splurge.

Each cottage is spacious, with high ceilings, polished concrete floors, wooden furniture and large windows -- you're close enough to the water that you can actually catch a sea breeze. Bathrooms are modern-meets-beach, with floor, walls, vanity and sink constructed with slate-grey polished concrete, the design softened with rustic bamboo accessories. The hot water shower has two showerheads. This is definitely not a weathered beach shack; guests also get a fridge, flatscreen TV, WiFi and air-con. The largest cottage includes a kitchen and living area.

The property itself doesn't have much space and the garden is tiny. In any case, you'll probably spend more of your outdoor-time on your bungalow's shaded terrace. Ms Kim is lovely and she goes out of her way to ensure guests are comfortable. Her English is excellent and the room rate includes breakfast and bicycle. This is a great pick for An Bang.

Red Flower Cottage Homestay is easy to find. There's a sign above their entrance way which is directly on the An Bang village road. As you approach the An Bang main parking area, head left on the paved road behind the beach.

An Bang Seaside Village

Though the room rates have gone upmarket since our previous review, they are still a reasonable offer for those who want solid bungalows that combine both beautiful and practical touches.

Those beautiful touches include a front terrace with sofas, cushions, tables and chairs, beachy decor and a small private tropical garden shared between the houses. The practical side means guests get air-con, ceiling fan, WiFi, kettle, spacious open-plan interiors, shelves for clothes, flatscreen TV and a polished concrete bathroom with hot water. The Mango House and Banana House, which has two queen beds, have an outdoor kitchenette; all room rates include breakfast.

These houses are designed to keep you comfortable and feeling at home in a quiet, private place whenever you aren't at the beach. By the way, the beach is just 67 steps away down a sandy lane that will deposit you on the quiet end of An Bang, away from the main concentration of eateries and beach chairs. Overall, this is for someone who wants a low-key beachside living experience in a neighbourhood-type setting.

With all the different houses, the pricing is confusing and the rate we saw on an online booking site was significantly cheaper than the walk in rate we were quoted.

An Bang Sunset Village Homestay

If flashpackers are willing to stretch their wallet, they can snag one of the four rooms in a modern building, located a short walk to the beach.

Rooms have more character and charm than your average joint. A wraparound walkway with seating and a communal terrace connects the upstairs rooms. Inside the exposed brick walls have been painted with a stylish grey-blue that compliments the warm terracotta floors, clean white linens and cherrywood-stained shelving. Tall folk will love the high ceilings.

Bathrooms are surprisingly swish, decked out in marble tile, contemporary fixtures, warm lighting and a separate shower area. It's all very elegantly minimalist and comfortably modern.

WiFi, air-con, breakfast and bicycle are included. You'll find this joint along the road lined with small shops and homestays. The lane is opposite the beachside, a few metres down the path behind a gate. To sweeten the deal, the owners have a restaurant on the beach and guests are free to use their chairs and umbrellas for free.

Nhu Que Vegetable Village Homestay

It has new dorms and one of the best value private rooms within reasonable distance to An Bang.

To get to An Bang, you'll take Hai Ba Trung Road and just before you reach the coast, the road runs right through Tra Que Village, an isle known for its many vegetable gardens and farms. Happily situated in the eastern tip of the isle is Nhu Que Vegetable Village Homestay and when we arrived, we found the owners busily shelling heaps of peanuts. This village is very much about growing good things to eat and earthy folk will love the sight of everyone industriously tending to their plants or harvest.

The quirkiness comes from the two very different types of accommodation to choose from: either a private room in the new, bland modern three-storey home or a dorm in a very charming traditional style building. The small private rooms are your typical Vietnamese guesthouse room, with air-con, WiFi, small flatscreen TV, table, chair and a sparkling tile wet-room bathroom with hot water shower. It would appeal to flashpackers.

The dorms have more character, atmosphere and are a great price. The wooden building, which is adorned with lanterns, has wooden doors, large windows and two rooms, one with five beds and the other with three. When we visited in May 2016, the building and the furnishings were all new, including the brand new mattresses still wrapped in plastic. There was an attached outdoor bathroom with shower, also brand new. The dorm is kitted with fans, electric plugs but no lockers. It's not as if this place will be hopping with guests though. The family doesn't speak English and for now, this homestay flies under the radar.

The room rate does not include breakfast. We spotted some bicycles so An Bang Beach and its many eateries are a good option for food, otherwise it is a 4.5

kilometre journey to the town. If you want a lively crowd or don't want to wake up to the sound of roosters in the morning, this is probably not the place for you. Budget traveller who enjoys rural scenes while being an easy bike ride to the sea, Nhu Que Vegetable Village Homestay is the spot.

The Hippie House

Located down a narrow alley at the edge of An Bang, this place has a chilled out, happy, bohemian vibe. Shells hang from the trees, guests write colourful messages on the walls and in between beach time, you'll find yourself hanging out on the front porch or in the communal kitchen where you're welcome to whip up your own meals.

Private rooms (shared bathroom) are basic but well-put together affairs, coming with a mosquito net, cupboard and fan, all a modern day hippie needs. There is also a gorgeous two-bedroom house available to rent. They've done an amazing job renovating an old

Vietnamese house into a beach-chic haven, keeping the existing patterned floor tiles and adding a sleek kitchen, high ceiling, shelves for clothes and outdoor bathroom. Keeping with the hippie credo, it's fan only. The place is simple yet has just enough comfort to satisfy flashpackers. It's beach living come true, and would be a steal if you're a group of four.

Under the Coconut Tree Homestay

Shaded by a swathe of (yes, you've guessed it) coconut trees, Under the Coconut Tree is home to cool wooden and tile ancient houses clustered around a solidly built communal dorm featuring 200-year-old timber.

It's got all those rustic touches an earthy beach-bum backpacker will love: well-cared for bamboo and thatch huts, rattan walls, outdoor showers and a shady bar/hangout area to relax. To be clear, there's no view of the ocean or beach, but it's a short walk down the lane.

Taking up the centre position is a huge open-air dorm house featuring solid wood bunks. Each comes with lockable under-bed storage, a light, two power outlets, a mosquito net and cotton bed linen. Roll-up windows and large ceiling fans keeps a slight breeze circulating, while a screened off ensuite bathroom houses five private toilet and shower stalls. The big open space keeps everything airy. The trade off is that there's not much protection from the noise, nor is there much privacy between the bunks.

If you're in need of privacy then splash out on a private room. Don't expect too much -- it's still quite rustic. Within the bamboo walls you get a bedside table, window, mosquito net, fan and an ensuite bathroom. What used to be a smaller five-bed dorm has been converted into a family room decked out with antique furniture, fans, polished timber floors, electricity and ceiling fan. WiFi is available, however, breakfast and bicycle in not included in the room rate.

Under the Coconut Tree is found in An Bang's cluster of cottages and homestays. When you arrive to An Bang's main parking via Hai Ba Trung Street, head left, down the road behind the beach. Look for the signposted narrow lane. There you will arrive at their reception/restaurant/lounge.

Under the Coconut Tree is the best backpacker option for An Bang Beach, and an attractive alternative to staying at a cramped, forgettable hostel in town. It would be easy to imagine a tiny community of backpackers strolling down the sandy lane to the beach and bonding over a few beers. Not surprising, this place is popular so book in advance.

An Bang Garden Homestay

Somehow the stark white walls, polished concrete floors and dark wood furniture works without feeling under furnished or clinical. Perhaps it's the sliding glass doors, providing a view to the neatly manicured lawn and tropical greenery that makes it work. In any case, travellers can look forward to rooms with chilly air-con, WiFi, sitting area, bedside table and plug, flatscreen TV and private porch. The bathroom is also heavy on polished dark grey concrete, including a purpose built concrete sink and countertop.

Overall, the details are not as tidy as they could be -- the unsightly plug for the fridge is above it high on the wall, the few pieces of framed art are awkwardly placed. It's also a slightly longer walk to the beach than An Bang Sunset Village Homestay (to find An Bang Garden Homestay, pass An Bang Sunset, continue south, then turn left down the paved lane). It's still a solid choice and not a bad place to use as your base for surf and sand.

Cua Dai Beach

Cua Dai Beach runs eight kilometres from the Cham island ferry port north to An Bang beach. Once the darling of Hoi An with its rough-grained white sand and restaurants and resorts, Cua Dai is now affected by severe coastal erosion and its disappearance has accelerated in recent years. Flash resorts have constructed their own protective walls and breakwaters; their rock walls aren't the most pretty sight and it's increasingly apparent that if your main purpose of staying at a resort is for the beach, this is not the place. Hotels here still deliver on the ocean views, swimming pool, restaurants and services -- however, expect a very small sized patch of sand, if any. Cua Dai has lost a bit of lustre but that means rates have dropped in recent years and there are discounts to be had.

Victoria Hoi An Beach Resort & Spa

The breezy high-ceilinged lobby has gorgeous details and the accommodation and service standards remain high. The rooms are split into two areas, with multiple-storey Mediterranean buildings at the rear of the resort and smarter duplex bungalows towards the water's edge. The buildings facing the garden or the road/river are well appointed, with cherry-wood flooring, simple and tasteful decor livened by dramatic accents, and classic modern hotel amenities: minibar, desk, luggage stand, flatscreen TV, WiFi and a generously sized bathroom with toiletries. High-end touches include fresh fruit and turn down service.

Of course, the junior ocean suites are the stunners and despite not being directly on the beach, it's still an amazing way to wake up in the morning to a view of the ocean. Open the sliding glass door for a fresh sea breeze and the sound of the waves. Junior suites come in two different styles: French colonial or Japanese zen. Both are comfortable and refined, with the added bonus of an outdoor shower and an oversized tub.

Like the rest of Cua Dai, coastal erosion has completely eaten away the front beach. Guests can head to a modestly sized empty patch of white sand adjacent to the property -- there's umbrellas, loungers and they clean it daily, though it certainly is missing the fun-in-the-sun ambience of a typical beach resort. If beachfront is what you dream, look elsewhere. Cua Dai's decline translates to savings and look out for online offers, you get a great deal for a solid four-star.

So, no beach, but so many other things to look forward to: the pretty palm-lined swimming pool, spa, bar and restaurant, and they have classic Ural motorcycles with sidecars to run guests to and from town -- they also offer day tours in them, a unique, cute and fun way to get around. They pad on other experiences: happy hours, a dinner with traditional dance show several times a week and a Sunday brunch, 490,000 dong per person or 690,000 dong including bubbly.

The pool, beach and outdoor dining is very seasonal and the value of staying here is questionable during cold, wet season (November to March). Those ocean view rooms may not be so pleasant with grey skies, big winds and waves. Other times of year, Victoria Hoi An Resort & Spa is an intimate, charming classic -- this is in stark contrast to the other Cua Dai hotels, including large group tour series hotel The Sunrise.

Cua Dai Street

Cua Dai Street runs for six kilometres from Hoi An town east, out to Cua Dai Beach. You'll need transport to town and it's also rather far from the ocean -- it isn't a great location so the only reason you'd want to stay here is for the property itself, which is why we've covered just four excellent hotels in the US$40-80 range and one good backpacker dig.

Hoi An Ancient House Village Resort & Spa

When we were warmly welcomed by the security guard, it was a great sign of good things to come at Hoi An Ancient House Village Resort & Spa. The welcoming feeling continued with the reception. In fact, without exception every staff we passed on the property, be it a gardener or housekeeper, paused what they were doing, looked us in the eye, warmly smiled and greeted us. In our experience, service attitude like this is a mirror to the entire resort experience. It was truly impressive and it is safe to say that guests can expect stellar service at this resort off of Cua Dai Road.

Surrounded by countryside, the 56-room property doesn't feel overly big or impersonal. The grounds are spacious yet intimate, the spaces filled in with lush tropical gardens that offer privacy to the multi-storey buildings. Rooms are of a high standard, a pleasant mix of classic and modern. Enter the room and in the upper landing, find yourself in the semi-open concept bathroom which includes an enormous freestanding tub, a separate toilet room and shower room. A few steps down lead to sleeping/living quarters with a comfortable bed, sitting area and balcony overlooking either the pool or garden. Rooms come with WiFi, air-con, kettle, hair dryer, desk, minibar, bedside table and plugs, and TV.

Both the generously sized pool and the restaurant overlook a rice paddy, reminding guests that they are removed from the busy town -- three kilometres to be exact, equidistant between the old town and Cua Dai Beach. The resort offers free bicycle and regular shuttles to the town and An Bang.

It's taken a few years for this resort to find its niche, but now that it has, it's unlike any other in Hoi An and at its current price, excellent value. And if you aren't convinced, as we left the security guard bid us a warm farewell. It certainly made us want to return.

Paddy's Hostel

If the large pool and hangout Irish pub on the ground floor doesn't entice you, then perhaps the tidy and clean rooms will. When we visited in 2016, the recently refurbished hostel sported air-con dorms and private rooms that are more comfortable and cool than the majority of Hoi An hostels in town.

The shared rooms are very civilised and spacious -- there are no bunks and the beds aren't crammed in. Double beds are also available in the dorms, which sport some cool touches like exposed brick walls, individual reading light, electric outlet and storage, and an ensuite bathroom with shower and another separate shower room. Along with the extra shared toilets and showers in the hallway, no need to worry about long waits for the facilities. All looked clean.

Private bathrooms are equally fresh and clean: white walls, white linens, air-con, WiFi, big bathroom with modern fixtures and windows with thick curtains.

There's plenty of space to hang out downstairs, whether guests want to quietly catch up on emails or to meet others. The ground floor pub has a billiard table, indoor and outdoor seating, picnic tables, pavilions and sun beds around the pool to laze around. Breakfast and five-hour bicycle rental is included in the room rate, sweetening the already good deal and making it easier to get on with the day.

Paddy's Hostel is located three kilometres from the old town and less than a kilometre from Cua Dai Beach, just before the bridge. While Cua Dai Beach main hub is severely eroded, journey up the coast towards An Bang and you'll find lots of undeveloped white sand to lie down on. An Bang itself is only four kilometres via the road along the coast.

Rock Villa Hoi An

The small hotel and its tropical gardens are sandwiched between a river and rice paddy, a resplendent sight when the fields are growing. This place is for those who want peaceful countryside over the tourist bustle of the old town.

Rock Villa's rooms are spacious, airy and well appointed with contemporary furnishings. They have a decidedly modern flair, balancing rough natural textures and sleek lines. For example, exposed brick walls are livened up with floating shelves and colourful vases. Firm mattresses are dressed with crisp white linens and all that natural daylight keeps everything light and bright. Creature comforts include air-con, flatscreen TV, a big bath/shower room and plenty of storage space. The best rooms are on the second storey and come with a choice of balcony or terrace.

Rock Villa is a great pick for families on a more modest budget. The upstairs has two interconnecting bedrooms, a shared bathroom and a wrap around balcony. Within the safety of the private walled garden, there's a grassy area and swings for kids. The 25-metre pool has a separate kids splash pool which and there are plenty of toys to keep the little ones entertained. Bicycle use is free and they have child seats and small bikes for older kids.

Very few restaurants or cafes lie within walking distance of Rock Villa but fortunately the family here have a very good Vietnamese restaurant on-site that also run cooking classes for guests on request. Dining locations are aplenty -- eat in the garden, by the river, poolside, in the large shared covered terrace or on your own balcony.

The nearest competitor to Rock's quirky style and quality finishes is An Bang Seaside Village, which is close to the beach but feels more like an independent vacation house, so there is less service and no pool. Rock Villa is a great choice for young families as it's quiet, safe and the staff look after you as if you were part of the family. There's a discount for stays three nights or longer.

Finding Rock Villa is difficult if you miss the sign. Look for 171 Cua Dai Road (approximately 1.5 kilometres from Cua Dai Beach) and you'll see Rock Villa's signpost. It's just 250 metres off of Cua Dai Road.

Muca Boutique Resort

There's no big draw to a Cua Dai Street location, which means hotels located here have to have work hard to entice prospective guests. Like Hoi An Ancient House Village, Muca Boutique Resort delivers and makes a good case for choosing to stay a little out of the way. This oasis offers excellent value.

The three-storey buildings of just 36 rooms is tucked away in the countryside at the edge of a small river, located in the same cute hamlet as Rock Villa. Rooms come in three categories and differ by size only.

All offer modern fittings, which perhaps is a slight let down considering the exceptionally pretty and charming old world exterior. However, the rooms are comfortable and we'd easily overlook the amateurish framed paintings on the wall because the beds are huge and get bigger the higher up the categories you go (premier room beds are the size of two queens), flatscreen TVs are huge, the bathrooms are modern and functional and large wardrobes come with a safe, robes, kettle and beach towels.

Superior garden level rooms are family friendly, giving an option of interconnecting rooms while deluxe and premier take up the balconied first and second floors.

Muca Boutique Resort is located east of Cua Dai Street, across the river. It's 1.5 kilometres from Cua Dai Beach and four kilometres from the old town. This is a place for quiet relaxation and contemplation. Party animals should look elsewhere.

The river view from the resort's restaurant and infinity pool is mesmerizing. A stilted relaxation deck above the lazily flowing river kitted out with loungers is conducive to listening to bird song, disconnecting and winding down. Less lazy but equally as relaxing are offered activities such as fishing, boating and cooking classes.

Villa Hoa Su -- Frangipani Village Resort

If you don't mind the slightly out of the way location just off of Cua Dai Street, three kilometres from both Hoi An town and Cua Dai beach, it makes for a serene retreat away from the madding Hoi An crowds.

The man behind Hoa Su was involved in the building of one of Vietnam's most exclusive resort, the Nam Hai. Now he's copied it in miniature here, using a few of the same finishings and design details. Rooms are small but everything is well laid out, with a raised sleeping area, sofa, flatscreen TV, minibar, desk, DVD player, air-con, WiFi and a jaw-dropping outdoor bathroom, complete with enormous marble tubs and rain shower. Each villa faces a lotus-dotted moat surrounding a lounge area/restaurant housed in a classic ancient house and a modest swimming pool. It's only big enough to float around in but seems to fit well with the location.

Hoa Su is a hideaway, an isolated and quiet spot with seven suites that are ideal as a couple's retreat or for small groups of friends. It never feels busy. You'll probably want to arrange a driver to take you down the dark maze of roads to town or the beach for food, so factor that into your budget. There is not much to keep children entertained for long unless they've got a few pals to muck around with. Rock Villa is a more kid friendly option.

Cham Island

Aside from Hammock Homestay (below), camping is available on the island. At Bai Chong, on the western side of the island, two kilometres south from the village Cham Restaurant charges 200,000 dong a night to rent a tent. This is by far the best beach camping option on the island and the restaurant can serve breakfast, lunch or dinner. There are also tents available to rent on Bai Ong, the beach a kilometre north from town. While this beach gets hundreds of day tourists, all shops close at 16:00 and by sunset it is completely deserted leaving you with no food options or company. We met a couple of backpackers who discovered this the hard way after paying 150,000 dong for a tent.

Visitors can still opt to do the basic homestay and you can easily find several once you get off the jetty and walk around Bai Lang village. The few we saw were a bit grim and long in the tooth. There are more homestay options in Bai Huong, the fishing village near the southern tip. They can be organised through Homestay Bai Huong, which helps travellers connect with one of nine small family homes with basic Western-standard facilities, set up to help the fishing villagers with tourist income. It's a fixed price system of 120,000 dong per person, per night, extra for meals.

Hammock Homestay or Dich Vu Luu Tru Cai Vong

It's a purpose-built, two-storey building and the rooms are narrow, yet have all you need: a bed decked with clean white sheets on a proper mattress, mosquito net, bedside table with lockable cabinet, a wetroom bathroom with cold-water shower, sink, toilet, mirror, towel and a few hooks. Get a room at the front for direct access to the front balcony. There's also a fan, which thanks to 24-hour electricity these days, can be used at night.

Hammock Homestay is located in the main village of

Bai Lang. It's 300 metres from the big jetty disembark, go right and follow the road along the water before turning left into one of the village's narrow laneways. Call the owner in advance and she can pick you up from the boat. The place is good value considering it's the island's best option.

There's a bicycle free for guests to use, good for a couple of the nearby beaches but difficult for anything further you'll really need to get a lift on motorbike or hire a boat. Give them enough notice and the owners can provide you with home-cooked meals, a good idea when it comes to dinner as most outlets shutter up early. They made us simple but delicious mi quang noodles. A heartier meal with meat, rice and vegetables can be prepared for 120,000 dong.

The owners are friendly, albeit pushy -- inevitably there's a referral to a friend's Hoi An tailor shop or hotel. They also happen to own Cham Restaurant with a tourist setup on Bai Chong Beach.

Quick Guide

Getting in

By plane

The nearest airport is in Da Nang which has domestic connections from Hanoi, Ho Chi Minh City and Hue with Vietnam Airlines and VietJet Air and some international flights from Bangkok, Singapore Siem Reap, Hong Kong, Cambodia (for Angkor Wat) and charter flights from China.

The best option to come from Da Nang airport is booking Grab car (you need to have an app and activated account) and sharing it with other travellers. It should cost around 400,000 dong for whole car.

A private car from airport to Hoi An] costs about USD13. Try with Da nang airport Private Transfer is one of the most reliable companies in Hoi An. This is one occasion where haggling to set a fixed price is cheaper than going by the meter, but good luck with this - despite clear signs everywhere listing fixed price fares to destinations including Hoi An (should be 400,000 dong, July 2015: this can be negotiated to a 320k fixed price if you appear to walk off a few times) most drivers seem unwilling to discuss a fixed price. Meters will typically run to around 450,000 dong. The Hoi An airport transfer is highly recommended, the cost is comparable with a taxi (about USD20) but a better car and professional service. The ride takes about 45min.

Hoi An Express is also one of the most reliable companies in Hoi An. From Danang airport to Hoi An costs USD 6 (Feb 2018) by air-conditioned shuttle bus (minibus).

There are also private cars from Hoi An to Hue Imperial city with English speaking driver. You can travel to Hue then come back Hoi An in 1 day with some highlights stop on the way.

By train
There is no railway station in Hoi An. The nearest is in Da Nang, which receives several trains a day from

Hanoi, Ho Chi Minh City, Hue, Nha Trang etc. Most travel agents and hotels can book a train ticket for you.

Da Nang Railway Station: 202 Hai Phong, Tan Chinh Ward, Thanh Khe District, TP Da Nang, Phone: + 84 511 375-0666.

To catch the public 'yellow bus' from the train station to Hoi An, exit the station, walk across the car park and continue straight out Hoang Hoa Tham road with the train station behind you. Shortly after you reach a cross road with a Pizza Hut on the opposite left hand corner. The bus stop is 50m left of Pizza Hut at 299 Le Duan road, a tailor's shop, with a blue and white sign for bus #01 and #09. Bus #01 for Hoi An passes by every 20 minutes until 6pm. Note—busses on this route routinely attempt to overcharge foreigners. The correct posted fare is 20k, but you may be asked to pay as much as 5x this amount. Conductors make an amusing effort to shield from tourists what the other passengers are paying. Politely pointing out the correct fare, posted inside the front door, will usually drop the price down to 30k (perhaps for this reason the conductor will tell you to get on via the rear door). Whether or not to hassle further for the real 20k is up to you. The ride terminates at the Hoi An bus station just outside the center.

The busstop has moved further down the road, keep on walking down Le Duan Rd until you see the next bus stop. You can also check the public transport route of Google Maps, as it shows the route of the bus. The current fare seems to be 25k. No further problems.

Cheap Taxi Option is with www.dichungtaxi.com. They offer private cabs for 220k or shared cabs option picking up other passengers on the way for 150k. Order from the website.

By bus
There are two different bus stations in Hoi An now (older guide books just show the one on D Hung Vuong)and the public buses to Da Nang leave from the station about 2km north west of the centre on Le Hong Phong.

A *xe om* from Hoi An bus station to the old town should be around 10-15,000 dong.

Between Hoi An and DaNang there is a yellow, public bus #1. It stops just outside Hoi An city centre (about 10 min walk) and runs thru DaNang centre (here it has several, market stops). As of February 2016 the price is 20.000 dong. The price is listed on the door and inside the bus. It may read 17k, but the updated correct fare is 20k. Text size vary, it may be in the back. The whole trip takes about 40-50 min. On the bus they try to charge foreigners 50,000 dong, or more (aka close to the price of private vans from a hotel in Hoi An to the airport in Da Nang). Locals may support the scam by pretending they are also paying 50,000 dong, insist on the fare and they will lower it to 30,000, insist and pay the official one. Expect no change if you have a 20,000 dong note. So; have exact change, stay calm, be polite, firm/unbudging and point to the pricetable. They will budge! Though it may not be pretty.

Beware of bus drivers putting your luggage at the front and sparing you the nicest front seat, likely they want you to pay 50,000 dong and threaten to kick you off (although they never will).

A good tip is to take photos of the fare chat on the outside of the bus before you get on. Once on the bus keep your bags close to you. When the fare collector comes around start video recording the transaction and make it obvious that you a recording them - a video is hard evidence and if reported they could lose their job. Politely offer a 20,000 vdn note and ignore any further requests for money. It does not cost any additional to have your bag on board, despite what they say (an obvious exception to this world be if you have large bags that are taking up seats etc).

Again they will budge and accept 20,000 vdn in order to save face. Do not get angry at them - stay calm and collected so that you don't lose face! Finally if they are genuine and do not even try to overcharge you, consider giving them a small tip! It's not about the money, it's the principle.

Buses are frequent - every 20 or 30min pick time, else every hour - so you can simply sit down, have a coffee, enjoy air-con while talking to nicer locals and then jump on the next bus. Same goes for Hoi An - Da Nang. The bus passes through downtown Da Nang and near the train station as well. If you come from Da Nang airport, the closest bus stop of the same route to Hoi An is at the roundabout where the streets Nguyễn Tri Phương and Điện Biên Phủ meet (a nice 10-15min walk, since you can walk along the lake). This bus stop is clearly marked with a road sign. Google Maps also shows the locations of bus stops for this route in Da Nang.

There are no shortage of travel companies and private buses travelling to and from from Hoi An to destinations such as Hue, Hanoi, Saigon, Dalat and Nha Trang.

Open-tour buses like Sinh cafe, Hanh Cafe, An Phu run daily up and down the coast from Da Nang and Hue taking 3.5-4h and priced at 60,000-100,000 dong (*Mar 2012*) and Nha Trang taking 9-10 hours overnight and priced at USD10-15 (*April 2013*).

By motorbike or taxi

It is easy to take a motorbike or taxi to and from Da Nang via the Marble Mountains (see below), from where you can catch a train onwards. This trip cost 460,000 dong from Da Nang bus station, by the meter in Jan 2013. From Hue or Quang Binh, you can take a private taxi to Hoi An. On the way, you will photo stop at Lap An Lagoon, Lang Co Beach, Hai Van Pass, Cham Museum. Taxi from Danang Airport to Hoi An centre is about 250,000 dong in general (as of July 2016). You can book at this price in most of the travel agency in Hoi An town. Some hotel might charge you more from USD 13 - 17

By boat

The old Champa way was to travel by the river system. The rivers of Hoi An cover hundreds of km and offer an interesting & adventurous alternative to travelling by road. Get on a boat and you'll begin to see a whole lot more of Hoi An and the Delta.

Get around

The centre of Hoi An is very small and pedestrianised, so you will be walking around most of the time. Motorbikes are only banned from the centre of town during certain times of day, so keep an eye out for them; even in the most narrow alleys. Evenings are especially busy with motorbikes two, or even three abreast competing with pedestrians for even the smallest space on the street!

The city's government does not allow motorbikes to enter the Old Town on the 14th and 15th of each lunar month. On those evenings, a lot of activities, including traditional games such as *bai choi*, *trong quan*, and *dap nieu* are held in all over the town.

By bike

You can easily get around on a bicycle to most of Hoi An's attractions, as motorcycle and car traffic is banned from the city center's tourist area during most daylight hours. You can use a bicycle to go the beach or reach some of the more remote hotels. It is easy and cheap to hire a bicycle (c. 20,000 dong per day in Jan 2013). For mountain bikes, head to Anh Cuoc shop, at 635 Hai Ba Trung.

Traffic in the area of Hoi An is minimal, so if you've been avoiding getting on a bike in the big cities, small towns and the surrounding countryside like Hoi An are ideal to get used to the road rules.

By taxi

Taxis can be found in the middle of Le Loi St, over the river on An Hoi or called by phone. When busy, taxis may refuse your fare back to your hotel from town if it is too close, opting for larger fares. Arranging a shuttle from your hotel may be a better option although prices can be higher. A local 15 minute taxi fare is around 60,000 dong.

Motorbike taxis, of course, are always an option. Some shops have electrical bicycles (especially along Duong CuanDai, close to the centre -75.000 dong, Jan 2013). You can also charter boats for about US$1/hour. Cost of motorbike rentals in Hoi An town was 80-100,000 dong in Feb 2013 although a hotel may charge double. You get a step-thru with auto clutch. These can handle two full sized adults easily enough. There are any number of small shops renting them, you will be offered a helmet usually. Take it every time - there are plenty of roadside helmet checks. Failure to wear one results in the bike being confiscated and a USD75 fine. Worse, you probably haven't got a Vietnamese driving license and there are no papers to sign, no agreements made so you are on your own legally.

Ride to the outskirts of Danang to visit the stunning Marble Mountains. If you look left from An Ban beach, you can see the Marble Mountains (3 prominent lumpy hills) clearly - the high rises further on are Da Nang. Bear in mind the total lack of signposts, and just keep looking left at the flat terrain until it isn't flat any more! You are on a dual carriageway road all the way. It's standard practice for the bike to have only enough gas to make it a few metres to the next gas station.

In addition to gas stations, there are also little hand-operated roadside pumps everywhere; these can be convenient, but they're more expensive. The proprietor may show you a sign with a few calculations for non-Vietnamese speakers such as 3 litres is 90,000 dong. You actually see the gas draining through a calibrated sight glass. In a commercial gas station they can, and do bang in half a tank then shut the machine off to serve someone else. The amount in money has gone from the display, and he tells you a totally made up figure. All this makes the roadside hand pump with sight glass a lot more foreigner friendly. Gas costs around 25,000 dong/litre and one litre is enough for sightseeing to the beach and back and zipping around town. If you take a trip - lets say you ride to My Son 2-up - then you will use about 4L. It's inevitable that you will get lost 5 times between Hoi An and and My Son! Luckily fuel is cheaper out in the countryside.

Important: foreign International Driving Licences are NOT valid in Vietnam and in case of accident, a foreigner driving a motorcycle without a valid licence is at fault and will pay! Also personal insurance may not be valid for someone riding on a motorcycle with a driver who does not have a valid license.

By boat

The old Champa way was to travel by the river system. The rivers of Hoi An cover hundreds of km and offer an interesting & adventurous alternative to travelling by road. Get on a boat and you'll begin to see a whole lot more of Hoi An and the Delta.

Seeing

To enter most of the main attractions in the Old Town (i.e. the handful of buildings that aren't shops) you require a ticket (120,000 dong), which is sold at various kiosks. You certainly do not (usually) require a ticket just to walk the streets. But it can seem that way since the main entrance to the Old Town is the Japanese covered bridge, which being one of the attractions /does/ require the ticket. But there's nothing to stop you using the nearby footway on the waterfront instead.

Piped (western, classical) music throughout the main old town streets adds to the crass Disneyland feel.

An "it's ok to rip off the foreigners" attitude is pervasive throughout Hoi An (much more so then in most Vietnamese cities). Cyclo drivers charge 300,000 Dong ($15 U.S.) for a ride that would cost less than 20,000 Dong ($1 U.S.) in other cities of Vietnam. Restaurants in the Old Town area are VERY expensive, charging four times what most restaurants would charge and serving portions that are half the typical size.

Once purchased, the old town ticket (120,000 dong) includes five coupons that can be used to enter five attractions of your choosing: museums, old houses, assembly halls, the handicraft workshop (and traditional music show) or the traditional theatre, and either the Japanese Covered Bridge or the Quan Cong Temple. Tickets are sold at various entry points into the Old Town, including Hai Ba Trung Street, and also at some of the attractions, including the Cantonese Assembly Hall. The city requests that visitors dress "decently" while visiting sites in the Old Town. Men should wear a shirt and women shouldn't wear bikini tops, sleeveless blouses or skirts above the knees. Respect the local culture and remember that you are not on the beach.

If you are not into visiting some fairly mediocre museums (see below for details), do not purchase the coupon or you will feel cheated - there is not much to see otherwise.

If you have the opportunity to visit a long-established Chinese expat community elsewhere in Asia - Malaysia, Singapore, Chinatown in any of the large cities of Thailand or the Philippines - consider skipping Hoi An entirely.

First, you may choose one of the two landmarks of Hoi An:

Japanese Covered Bridge's Pagoda (Chua Cau or Lai Vien Kieu). The Bridge is located on the west end of Tran Phu Street, but the ticket is ONLY required to access the annexed pagoda on one side of the bridge's interior; the bridge itself is free for crossing. The bridge was constructed in the early 1600's by the Japanese community, roughly 40 years before they left the city to return to Japan under the strict policy of sakoku enforced by the Tokugawa Shogunate, and renovated in 1986. Today, it's the symbol of Hoi An.

Precious Heritage Museum, 26 Phan Boi Chau, 0510 6558 382, . A 250m2 display of photos and artifacts collected by Réhahn during the past 5 years of the french photographer's explorations of Vietnam. Free Entrance.

Quan Cong Temple, 24 Tran Phu Street.

The ticket allows admission to four museums in the Old Town (one ticket-one museum):

Museum of Folk Culture, 33 Nguyen Thai Hoc Street. Some may be put off by the bizarre-looking plaster sculptures of Vietnamese peasants, but this museum documents the dress and culture of rural Vietnam.

Museum of Trade Ceramics, 80 Tran Phu Street. The dusty, unlabeled displays of broken pottery are eminently forgettable, but the house itself is nice enough, and it provides a better opportunity to explore the shape and layout of an old Hoi An home than you'll find at any of the Old Houses (below).

Hoi An Museum of History and Culture, 7 Nguyen Hue Street. The museum contains some old black and white photos of Hoi An taken in the early 20th century. It also houses an old canon, some two-thousand year old pots from the Sa Huynh period, and a case full of 9th century bricks and tiles from the Champa period.

Museum of Sa Huynh Culture, 149 Bach Dang Street. The museum's main collection consists of pottery and urns from the 1st and 2nd centuries. Upstairs, there used to be another museum, the Museum of the Revolution. Its main collection consists of pictures from war heroes and a collection of weapons such as grenade launchers, machine guns and AK47s. However, this collection has now been relocated to the new museum building at the top of Le Loi Street, and is not currently open to the public.

There are three old houses that exist in an awkward halfway state between museum show-piece and somewhat shabby residence for the family that lives there.

Phung Hung House, 4 Nguyen Thi Minh Khai Street, just west of the Japanese Bridge. Traditional two-story wooden house, inhabited over 100 years by eight generations; and the current one attempts to guide you around in hope of a tip.

Quan Thang House, 77 Nguyen Thai Hoc Street.

Tan Ky House, 101 Nguyen Thai Hoc Street. As above, a younger member of the family will provide a cup of tea and a "tour" that doesn't stray from the front room of the house, as you'd need to step over sleeping members of the older generation to go anywhere else. The design of the house shows how local architecture incorporated Japanese and Chinese influences. Japanese elements include the crab shell-shaped ceiling supported by three beams in the living room. Chinese poems written in mother-of-pearl are hanging from a number of the columns that hold up the roof.

Numerous congregation halls, where Chinese expatriate residents socialized and held meetings, are dotted about the town. They are typically named after the home region of their members, such as Fujian and

Canton. Some do not have ticket-takers, so it's up to your conscience if you want to try wandering into a second.

Cantonese Assembly Hall (Quang Dong), 176 Tran Phu Street. Built in 1885, it has a calm courtyard with ornate statuary. Take a peek at the half-hidden back yard and its kitschy pastel dragon statues.

Hokien (Fujian) Meeting Hall (Phuc Kien), 46 Tran Phu Street. Built in 1757.

Chinese All-Community Meeting Hall (Trieu Chau), 157 Nguyen Duy Hieu. Built in 1887. It's near the Fujian hall, also spanning the block.

Finally, you can choose one of the following to get some "Intangible Culture":

Hoi An Handicraft Workshop, 9 Bach Dang Street. Folk music performances are offered at 10:15 and 15:15 every day except Monday. The performances last about 20 minutes.

Traditional Theatre, 75 Nguyen Thai Hoc Street.

Swan Boats on the river near the footbridge. Make sure you check out the swan boats on the river. These are literally passenger boats shaped like giant swans whose eyes light up at night and which play 'Santa Claus Is Coming To Town' at double speed.

Doing

Hire a motorbike to Hue You can hire a motorbike all over Hoi An, but MotorVina have offices in Hoi An, De Nang and Hue and offer a free emergency recovery service (or will pay for a local mechanic to fix what needs fixing). For $2 extra they will transport your luggage to their office in Hue so you can ride freely! They will also pick you up from your accommodation in Hoi An for free to get you to their office. We organised it through our hostel and paid $15/person (not including luggage transport) so I'm sure it can be negotiated down from this.

Hoi An address: 482 Cửa Đại, Minh An, Tp. Hội An, Quảng Nam 560000, Vietnam

Long-tail boat, kayak or small round boat (thúng) rides down the river. Mr. Phap (0906 416 433) offers round boat rides through the water coconut groves for 1-2 ppl, 50k/person/hour (anything you'd pay beyond that price is just others' commissions). You can see some wildlife living in the shallow waters, and he might even make you a leaf hat! Address: To 2 Thon Van Lang.

Walk around the old town at night. The most popular activity to do is actually quite simple; as sundown approaches until 21:30, the old town lights up with lanterns and other lights and attracts window shopping and peaceful evening walks. The majority of activity happens in the old town during this time window when the temperature is cooler, and is a great time to stroll around and explore shops, restaurants, people watch, and simply soak in the beauty of Hoi An. The street lanterns shut down approximately 21:30 and vendors and food stalls follow suit in the following hour. By around 22:30, most vendors, bars, and restaurants are closed with only late night bars and a few food stands remaining.

{{infobox|Cua Dai Beach|Please note as of Jan 2016 there was a coastal erosion and the sandy beach was washed away. In 2017, the beach was nourished and some resorts here still have the sandy beach for beach activities, swimming etc.

Play or relax at the beach - Although it is situated 4km away, the beach north east of old town (An Bang) is a popular place to go for a swim, splash in the water, eat food from vendors that serve food under the shade of palm trees that overlook the beach, or at night to eat at one of the many seafood restaurants that also offer beach views. As in the old town you'll be mobbed here by touts selling food or charging you to park your bike.

Cinnamon Sunset Dinner Cruise. It's hard to beat cocktails on the water at sunset and the Cinnamon Cruise takes it to a new level: attentive waiters, white table cloths, first-rate food; charming solid wooden junk offering river views of one of the prettiest towns in the world all interlaced with twilight's magical hues dancing over the Thu Bon River, Cinnamon Cruises.

Kayaking. For those looking to get out and enjoy the outdoors, kayaking is a fun, easy, and enjoyable activity that everyone can do from Hoi An. Get a chance to immerse in nature paddling through a maze of water coconut palm forest, and watch the everyday river life of local fishermen. Relax and sit in a kayak while watching the sunset over the river. Guided tours and rental are available. Tour price starts from $25 per person, Hoi An Kayak Tours.

Tra Que Village, (around 2km from Hoi An centre, turn in from Hai Ba Trung street). Tra Que is a picturesque, green and clean vegetable village where most veggies served in dishes throughout Hoi An are grown. Take a day to discover the calm rural life in this area of Hoi An. The guys at Onetrip offers a wonderfully unique village tour if you are interested, where you can escape the busy city life and cycle around the countryside on a bicycle and later, paddle along the De Vong river on a wooden sampan. Interact with the farmers, get down and dirty and pick your own veggies and later, use them to cook your own meal. You can go fishing too - Tra Que Village has it all.

Pottery Village, Tra Que Village and Lantern Making Factory. A great combination between biking, countryside sightseeing and cultural visiting. This bike tour will lead you through a peaceful countryside to a Pottery Village, Tra Que vegetable Village and a traditional lantern making shop where you will see how pottery and lanterns have been made for generations, and try tasty meal at local farm.

You could also Rent a motorbike. If the traffic scared you in Ho Chi Minh or Hanoi, here is the place to learn. Note: foreign International Driving Licences are NOT valid in Vietnam and in case of accident, etc, a foreigner riding a motorcycle without a valid licence is at fault and financially will pay! Also personal insurance may not be valid for someone riding pillion on a motorcycle with a rider who does not have a valid licence.

Cham Island Diving has been operating from Hoi An since 2002. The international team offer daily boat and speedboat tours to Cham Island for scuba diving and snorkelling activities. Boat tours can be booked at our Dive Bar and restaurant in Hoi An old City where our diving and snorkelling team will be happy to help you, regardless of your ability or experience.

The Kianh Foundation, 61 Phan Chau Trinh Street, on the corner of Le Loi Street ((inside Go Travel Vietnam)), . A UK charity that has worked in Hoi An since 2001, providing health and education services to disabled children. Kianh delivers its specialist services from its purpose-designed Day Centre in Dien Ban district, 10 minutes outside Hoi An. Dien Ban was heavily bombed during the war with America and has over 1,000 children with disability who do not have access to essential services. Visit their Hoi An office to find out more about their work and how you can help to make a difference.

Hoi An Silk Village, 28 Nguyen Tat Thanh Street, +84 5103 921144, Daily 09:00-21:00. Revived 300 year-old Champa silk traditions - half day tours encompassing the entire silk process, from silkworm to dress making. Converted an ancient Quang Nam style house into a showroom of 100 different ao dai, representing all 54 different minority groups in Vietnam. Also a spacious colonial-style restaurant serving local menu items and a silk showroom where professional tailors custom design and make garments for visitors. * Cham islands are 15km from Cua Dai. There are seven islands altogether named according to their shape or characteristics. Good for diving, snorkelling, and sightseeing. USD19.

Cham Island Snorkeling tour Sea Trek VietNam is specialize in tour in Cham Island by wooden boat. Our tour begins at Cua Dai wharf by Vietnamese traditional boat. The Boat has 48 seats, the jouney takes about 1 hours. On the deck, you have time for relaxing, sight seeing. At the location, the Guests can swim, snorkel. The towels are prepared for all the guest.

You will move to Bai Chong beach to relax and have a lunch. ffter lunch, guests can swim or just relax in the hammocks. The tour finish around 3 pm. Not many tour to Cham island by Wooden boat as Sea Trek tour.

My Son Sanctuary (*My-Son-Sanctuary*), My Son. 5. Learn about the rise and fall of the once formidable Champa Kingdom See eight century's worth of sculptural masterworks. Typically, travelers go on a guided tour by bus or boat,

motorcycle tour that will take travelers into the nearby villages to understand more about the local culture, dating back to the very beginning of the Nguyen Dynasty. The same people who made drums for the Nguyen lords are now converting war remnants into musical instruments. This tour is off the beaten path on a motorcycle. 15.

Watch sunset on Thu Bon River. A cruise down the Thu Bon river is one of the best ways to idle away an hour or two when in Hoi An. As for the best times to cruise: romantics and photographers should hit the Bach Dang docks for sunset, so start your trip at 16:45. Price is USD5-7/h.

Hoi An Blind Massage, 402 Cuai Dai (on the road to the beach, little building on the left just before Mercure hotel). 8am to 10pm. Professional and clean place, you can get a full body massage for USD5 (100,000 dong). The staff can understand if you want softer or harder, and they will ask you if it is OK during the massage. They have real massage beds and they put clean blankets on them in front of you. USD5.

The Timeless, 57 Tran Phu, Hoi An, Quang Nam-Da Nang, +84 510 391 9293, . 07:00-23:00. Opened to provide a comfortable and convenient stop for visitors walking and shopping in town. You can lay there for free, take tourism information, learn about Hoi An history, borrow a book, use their toilets, buy drinks (free water) and use Wi-Fi.

Vinahouse Space (Vinahouse Museum), km 950 Highway 1 A, Dien Ban District, Quang Nam Province, Vietnam (about 7 km outside Hoi An, on the highway to My Son), 0903 858 777, . 8a.m. to 5:30 (museum) 6 a.m. to 8 p.m. (Restaurant). Vinahouse Space is Vietnam's largest Museum of Architecture, with numerous houses from the 18th to the early 20th century preserved and relocated within its Feng Shui gardens. Museum is dedicated to both the architecture as well as the furnishings and implements of these houses. The restaurant features traditional cuisine from Central Vietnam, with everything made fresh in house. The grounds also feature a craft center, where wood carving and traditional cooking methods can be enjoyed. With 5 National Awards, one world record, and peaceful surroundings, Vinhaouse Space provides a unique opportunity to learn about Vietnamese architecture, food, and culture USD 5 (Museum).

SeaTrek - Snorkeling Tour (SeaTrek VietNam), 160A Nguyen Duy Hieu Street, +84902333010, . 8. A trip for relaxing with swimming, snorkeling and "Walking underwater". During "Walking underwater" adventure, fish of all shape and colours, local marine life will surround you. You will have a delicious lunch and relax at the Unique ecological Bai Chong beach of a Word Biosphere Reserved Cham islands recognized by UNESCO. Experience the adventure on VietNamese wooden boat with free coffee. 40-60.

Spa

Ginger Spa, 115 Cua Dai (near Fullmoon restaurant), +84 510 652 4579, . 08:00-21:00. combines ancient Vietnamese herbal treatments and steam baths with traditional massages to pamper and revive the weary tourist. This is an all natural traditional spa in a rural setting close to the centre of Hoi An. USD10-30.

Na Spa (Hoi An - Na Spa), 463 Cua Dai Street (on the way to the beach to your right), +84 510 391 4199, . Na

Spa is one of the premier spas in Hoi An. You'll find many pop up spas around town but Na Spa is one of the first spa chains that became successful quickly for their cleanliness and quality of work. They've recently built a Spa Villa that's worth checking out for the view.

Cooking Class

Cookly Dao Tien Cooking Class, 19/04 Phan Boi Chau, Hoi An, Vietnam, +845103454996 (), . The class is a combination of Vietnamese daily activities. Starting by driving to Tra Que village to see how Vietnamese people grow their vegetables. Also, visiting a market in Hoi An to understand Vietnamese herbs and spices. Once you arrive, put your apron on and get ready to master the art of Pho. VND 1,224,615.

Learn

Cooking lessons are offered at several restaurants around town. If you enjoyed your meal there, it can't hurt to inquire. There are also several established cooking schools with good reputations including "Rice Drum", "Morning Glory" and "Red Bridge" who offer a variety of courses ranging in price US$16-55. In any of these "good reputation" schools, as a hands on experience, you can only learn as far as how to chop the vegetables, assemble ingredients, and go through the cooking process. While a demonstration is held on what ingredients are needed, some of the basic sauces or flavoring is given to you pre-made. A different approach is to inquire in a restaurant where you eat if they can arrange a cooking class for you; in smaller establishments the cost will be lower ($10-$20 USD) and more intimate though less organized. Another option is simply asking if you can observe the cooking process once you order your food. For example, at the "Green Moss" restaurant, just walk in around midday or in the evening, choose 2 dishes, and you can watch them prepare it while you take notes on how to do it. The cook's explanations are good, and it's quite an efficient way for only USD2 (in addition to the cost of the dishes). The kitchen looks chaotic, but the food is really good.

Lifestart Foundation Painting and Lantern Making Classes, 77 Phan Chu Trinh, +84 167 355 9447, . Lifestart Foundation offers a unique, half day (morning or afternoon) tour including a traditional painting class with a local artist, Hoi An lantern making class, boat ride on the Thu Bon river and the chance to talk one-on-one with community artisans from disadvantaged backgrounds. Lifestart Foundation is a registered, grass-roots charity that helps disadvantaged Vietnamese people and their families become self-sufficient. All tour proceeds are used to support Lifestart Foundation's philanthropic projects in Vietnam.

Buying

One tourist trap all shoppers in Hoi An must know is that almost everybody earns commission from referring buying customers to shoes and tailor shops.

The standard commission rate paid by tailor shops to every receptionist, door boy, taxi drivers, hotel bus drivers, staff of 5 star resorts or any random stranger is 35%. Some of those "highly recommended" stores can appear popular, crowded and even offer cheap prices, but in reality are only pure shop fronts that leverage on cheap but low quality outsourcing.

Custom made Suits
Few tailors namely BeBe Tailor, Vanda Tailors, Yaly Couture and Thu Thuy have their in-house production and do not outsource. Most tailor shops are not actual tailors but more of store front owners. In every tailor shop, you can choose the colour and material, and dictate every part of the style. Measurements are taken and the specifications are either sent out for fabrication at a factory or workshop outside the city or rarely made in-house.

The suit is usually complete by the next day, though for best results there is then a second (or even third) fitting, when they adjust the suit to more accurately suit your body and tastes. Most shops will keep tailoring it until you are satisfied.

If there are no tailors working in the shop or if the store is not able to show you the details or components that goes inside a suit, most likely the tailor store front is outsourcing and do not have their own production

While outsourcing is economical for store fronts as the shop only pay a set price for each item made, many tailor shop owners that outsource have no idea about the construction techniques, the consistency, the interior details such as threads, interlining, canvassing, shoulder pads, buttons etc. The quality that is put out is obviously variable, uncontrolled and as a general rule quite low. The actual tailors want to maximize profit and use the cheapest materials available to make the end product. Corners are also cut as payment is made per piece; the more pieces you stitch, the more money you earn, which obviously compromises quality.

There is typically no elaborate, multiple fitting and re-fitting process with most of these tailors. If not specifically requested, you will most likely only ever deal with shop owners who outsource the actual tailoring work to sweat shops in the outskirts of town, and who may not even know how to or care about translating your fitting requests to the actual people doing the work. Outsourcing tailoring work also means that shop owners have a strong incentive to minimize additional fittings and rework as it will cut into their profit margins.

Caveat emptor - and remember where you are: there is no trade association, Office of Fair Trading or similar to complain to if you are not happy.

If you do insist on getting something done, below are a couple of hopefully helpful tips how to approach the situation. Getting tailored clothes done in Hoi An can be a fun and budget-friendly experience, just be sure to know what to expect and how to minimize the risk of being taken advantage of. Come prepared with a healthy dose of scepticism when listening to the sales pitch and make sure that the shop's interests are aligned with yours. Make sure that you have leverage to get refitting work done until you are happy (see below). Do not just rely on sweetly smiling shop assistants and their promises - there is usually a clear inverse relationship between the friendliness of their tone and how much money you have already parted with:

-*Pre-pay as little as possible:* Paying a significant deposit takes away the only leverage you have with shop owners to facilitate multiple 'real' fittings with tailors present. Shop owners will ask for significant or even full pre-payment to 'cover upfront costs', 'buy cloth', 'pay staff', 'cover urgent hospital bills for the ill grandmother', etc. Customers should resist this as much as possible. While it may not be easy to get the prepayment down to zero (not impossible, though), never pay more than ~25%. If the shop refuses, simply walk out and find a more reasonable one. Paying more will greatly reduce the shop's incentive to deliver a product which you are truly happy with: Deposits are never returned if the customer is not happy with the product. If you decide not to buy a substandard piece but have already paid most of the price, the shop will simply sell your clothes to the next customer, after some alterations, and keep your money - effectively selling the clothes twice.

-Stand your ground and ask for rework if you are not fully satisfied. Politely, but clearly and repeatedly state that you will not pay for the piece if rework is not done to your satisfaction (note, however, that this will only work if you have not already paid a significant deposit - see above). Don't hesitate to deliver this message in a confident voice, especially if other potential customers are within earshot. Also, insist on having the tailor doing the actual work present at all fittings. Make this clear on your first visit. If unhappy with the results of fittings, insist on going to the tailor's workshop for final alterations until you are happy. This may be resisted as

workshops are typically squalid affairs which shop owners don't want their usually Western clients to see (Yes, your tailored clothes are really only that cheap because you are taking advantage of extremely low wages in Vietnam.).

-Know what you want, bring samples of what you like and check every piece thoroughly: It is always a good idea to know in advance which 'specs' you want for your custom clothes (collar shape, cuff type, monograms, etc for shirts, for example). Bring a list if necessary. If you have something more unusual done and order multiple pieces, have them do one piece first and check that you like what you see. It helps a lot to bring a piece of your clothing where you like the cut or which has some obscure detail you would like replicated. Do not assume that local tailors are familiar with the intricacies of bespoke tailoring and the myriad of options and customization available which a more traditional tailor is familiar with and can advise you on. It is also a good idea to have the shop confirm to you in

writing what you have ordered, including all the specs and prices you have agreed upon. Finally, when you receive the product make sure to check that all the details have been done as agreed - on every piece.

-Quality has its price, including in Hoi An: If you go for the cheapest shop or cloth on offer you will be disappointed. Choosing a good suit is not just about comparing prices. Workmanship and what goes into the suit can largely vary. This does not mean, however, that you should not negotiate. It's part of the experience.

-Bring enough time and don't go for the 24h-suit (unless you want to look like a clown): You will need at least a few days for proper fittings. Let the shop owner know that you have enough time to come in multiple times. A negotiating tactic may involve being vague on your departure date - once more unscrupulous shop owners know when you need to leave they might string you along and not invest their time and money for proper fittings.

-Obviously, shop around*, do some on-line research or get personal recommendations before making a financial commitment.

-Get a receipt and keep it: This can be helpful if some eager customs inspector at your home airport decides to query you about how much your custom made clothing has cost as he may suspect that you are above the duty-free limit.

Simon The Tailor (*Bespoke Tailoring*), 02 Le Loi Street, +84935021431 (), . 9:00-21:00. Simon The Tailor- a family run business since 1995 and is one of the famous tailors for Suit & Shirt made with commitment to Quality, Service, Value. Staffs are friendly, professional, know exactly their stuffs assisting clients the whole process of choosing the right fabric to fitting. A wide selection of fine materials is available in store making this tailor more beloved. Price is fare, 100% refund guarantee for a flawless experience. From 20 USD.

Vanda Tailors (*Hoi An Tailors*), 631 Hai Ba Trung Street, +84984488811 (), . 8:30-21:00. Vanda Tailors- one of the few professional tailor shop that have their in-house tailors. All their suits are constructed with lapel roll, using genuine horsehair canvas unlike many tailors in Asia. Customer can view their production in their shop premises upon request. Prices are also transparent and very reasonable.

Remy Tailor Hoi An, 544 Cua Dai Street, +84 905405035 (). 08:00-21:00. Remy Tailor Hoi An is a Family Business within walking distance of Old Town, They have an extensive catalogue of suits and dresses to choose from, And also specialize in Copys: You can show them a photo of a garmet and they will reproduce it. They allow multiple fittings until you've got the perfect fit. Excellent customer service and they'll provide coffee or water whilst you browse their works. They also know all the ins and outs of Shipping and Exporting if you're buying bulk product.

B&K Bao Khanh Silk Tailor, 101 Tran Hung Dao street, +84 3510 861 818 (). 08:00-21:00. Bao Khanh Silk is an obscure, as although it is located on the main street of Hoi An, is outside the core of the city where all the tailors focus. Bao Khanh Silk has an impressive collection of dresses for women, reserved for special occasions than designs that may have wool. One of the points strong Bao Khanh silk are dresses tailor-made for women, as drawbacks and would say that the price is similar to its competitors

Cloned clothes

Hoi An has a long tradition of copying and then rapidly making up new garments for travellers.

You can bring in clothes (or even a picture of clothes) that you want copied to any tailor shop and they will try to imitate it. You can often choose the type of fabric and the colour for the copy. You can bargain for a better price, especially if you are getting multiple copies.

Bargaining when having custom clothes made: Custom clothes will cost more than ready-made in Vietnam, but should not cost anywhere near as much as in North America/Europe/Australia. You should aim for a fair price, with which both you and the shop owner are happy. If you are not happy with the price, you can go to one of the multitude of other stores in the city; if they are not happy, or feel you are being unfair in your negotiations, there is a chance they will not try as hard to make sure you are satisfied with the result.

When you first see the exterior of the Hoi An Cloth Market, a squat building that has seen better times, your first inclination will be to make like Usain Bolt and, well, bolt. Especially when you spy the mouldy green interior walls. But resist that impulse and bravely make your way through this warren of small stalls.

Custom made shoes
All the shoe shops in Hoi An will make custom shoes for you. The greatest concentration of shoe stores is along Hoang Dieu street, where there are at least eight

(small) stores in a row. You can ask them to make you a style that you see there, or one in a catalogue or picture. You can choose the material, colour and type of base. While some shops may work from conventional sizing, most will simply trace an outline of your foot and take some measurements. As with the custom clothes, the fabrication is usually done a little outside of town, or at least in an area with lower rent costs.

Roni Shoes & Handbag Shop (*Made To Measure*), No 60 Street 18/8, +84968060505 (). 09:00-20:00 daily. Roni Shoes Shop is renowned as the best shoes and bag maker in Hoi An with his excellent skills, high quality and great service. His staffs are friendly, no pushy, well knowledge help you to know what will work with each style. All products are perfect cut, handmade following clients' requirements,using real cow leather, price is also reasonable. Specially they offer 100% refund policy for any products not meet your expectation.

Friendly Shoe shop, 18 Tran Phu Streett, +84 935 211 382 (). 08:00-21:00. Friendly Shop shop is famous for its unique service. NO LIKE = NO PAY is their slogan. They import leather, zippers and buckles which make the quality much different

WARNING: Not all the shops are reliable and willing to refund your deposit if you are not satisfied with their work. Agree on a small deposit, if they are confident on their skills they will agree too. Asking if they will be able to make the shoes as required is not enough, because consistently with the local mindset about *not losing face*, they will never say "no, we don't have the know-how to make your shoes this or that way". So be extremely specific, don't forget to mention the colour of the stitchings (unless you like the stitching with a different colour from the leather). Ask them about the base, or you'll get a leather shoe with a plastic base cloned from some brand, and even if they trace the outline of your foot, you may find a different sized base, because they don't actually make the base custom sized. If you are not satisfied and want your deposit refunded, the shop attendants may start being aggressive and verbally abusing. The police are not going to enforce your "rights" (naively assuming you have any, as a foreigner customer). This warning is based on a negative experience at Lộc Phước, 45 Trần Phú Street, Hoi An.

Eating

There are three dishes that Hoi An is particularly famous for:

Cao lầu, a dish of rice noodles which are not quite as slippery as pho and a bit closer in texture to pasta. The secret is the water used to make it, and authentic cao lau uses only water from a special well in the city. The noodles are topped with slices of roast pork, dough fritters, and this being Vietnam, lots of fresh herbs and veggies.

White rose (banh bao vac), a type of shrimp dumpling made from translucent white dough bunched up to look like a rose.

Wonton dumplings ("Hoanh Thanh"), essentially the same as the Chinese kind, served up in soup or deep-fried.

The Central Market is a large building whose interior serves primarily as a place for food vendors. The vendors offer food all day starting in the morning. Seating on stools, eating a bowl of Cao Lau with wooden chopsticks, and sipping the ice cold "White Coffee with vinamilk" is an adventure. However, be warned that it is standard procedure for all food vendors to approach you immediately on entrance and try aggressively to have you sit at their stall.

If you wish to avoid choosing, a particular stall that serves Cao Lau has garnered the praise of Anthony Bourdain and is generally known as one of the best places in town. It can be identified by said label placed on the pillar behind the stall. Prices will vary atrociously, as shopkeepers swarm over you to sell you things, or even shove plates of food before you. Just keep declining politely and return the food if you don't fancy it. Keep small denominations of dong with you, as you probably won't get change if you give them US$. Also, confirm the prices before you partake of the food. Prices range from about 7000-20000 dong for a bowl of Cao Lau noodles, and 5000-7000 dong for a coffee. The baguette is a nice snack, and should not cost more than 10000 dong. You can point and say yes or no to the vegetables and chilli that they will add. Mineral water is around 10000 dong for a big 1.5L bottle.

Walking along the river at night, you will find a lot of pubs. Beer is around 30000 dong. Cocktails are around 20000-50000 dong. There are some bar foods available, such as fried prawn crackers for around 15000 dong a plate. Just walk into any pub and have a seat. Keep an eye out for "fresh beer" signs in some bars and restaurants; they sell very chilled glasses (probably half pint) of beers at the ridiculously cheap prices of 3000 to 5000 dong. These beers are produced by Viet A Breweries and are quite good. Do also look out for "Happy Hour" boards too.

Avoid the riverside cafe called Cafe Can. The cafe has the worst reviews of any in town. Customers complain about appalling service.

Madam Phuong bread (*banh my phuong*), 2B Phan Chau Trinh.. Open 6:30 AM and close 10:00 PM.. considered by many inside and outside of Vietnam to be the best Banh Mi in all of Vietnam. The banh mi was featured on an episode of Anthony Bourdain's "No Reservations". In particular, the Banh Mi Thit (pork) menu item has been recommended by many. Considering the level of international praise it has garnered, it would be a very recommended stop for anyone who wants to try authentic, good food. Price 20,000 dong..

Bamboo Buddha restaurant and lounge, On Nguyen Hoang St, An Hoi islet, 510 392 5000, . 14-23. A nice colonial building housing a French/international restaurant. Specialties include roasted chicken, australian steaks, foie gras, duck magret and more.Sangria, cocktails and an eclectic wine list compliment this trendy venue. 5-25$.

Quan Nho, 195 Pham Ngu Lao (A side street off Cua Dai). Down an alley off Cua Dai, there's some cheap, delicious rice at Quan Nho. Approx $2 for 2 people.

Cafe 99 (Close to Watering Hole Bar), 99 Tran Cao Van Street. Small eclectic cafe run by an extremely friendly owner named Long. Good coffee and atmosphere, awesome ca phe sua da (vietnamese iced coffee) $1, amazing staff.

Vegan/ Vegetarian
Minh Hien Vegetarian Restaurant, 50 Trần Cao Vân, . 09.00-22:00. Nice menu of vegetarian dishes, they also offer cooking classes. Friendly staff. budget.

Karma Waters, 213 Nguyen Duy Hieu (Centre of Hoi An, opposite An Phu hotel), 510 3927632, . 10.00-21:00. vegan (100% vegetarian) Vietnamese, International & Indian food. Juices & smoothies. Cooking classes & tours. This place is on the expensive side. $2.5 for a bowl of noodles soup with vegetables. $1.5 for orange juice. However, the food is good and the staff nice mid range.

The Joi Factory, Block 1, Tra Que Village (it's located inside Christina's Hoi An), on the way to An Bang Beach, . 09.00-22:00. The owners are vegetarians and therefore made sure that most dishes have a vegetarian version. So it's like a vegetarian restaurant where your meat-eating friends won't have to starve. It's a great balance of Vietnamese flavors and genuine hospitality. $5-$10.

Budget
Prices in the very centre of Hoi An are generally a little inflated by the tourist trade - An Hoi island is no longer the bastion of cheap street stalls that it once was; or if

it ever was. The tourist trade has really hurt the prices of all areas of town. Don't pay more than 10,000 dong for a baguette; 10,000 dong for a beer (most places want 10-15,000 dong); and 20,000 dong for a bowl of noodles. Look for the signs "FRESH BEER" -it's a glass (300mL) for 4,000 dong up. Great value. Bike towards An Bang beach and check out some of the street side restaurants for some cheaper eats.

The Balance Café, 02 Tran Quang Khai, : +84 (0) 510 3623 777, . The Balance Café offers Vietnamese food with innovative flavors made of fresh local products. It also serves very good vegetarian dishes and there are also really delicious cocktails made with fresh fruit juices. Vietnamese drip coffee, Espresso, cappuccino and latte are served at the the Balance Café and take away. Free Wifi, A/C dining room, outdoor dining spaces on all three floors with flowers and plants. The atmosphere is very relaxed with a modern, colorful interior design.Prices are reasonable and worth. 110k-250k.

Cafe Zoom Hoi An, 134 Tran Cao Van, +84 510 392 6626, . 7:00 am - 11:00 pm. The place to go to for a break from Vietnamese food. Very good fajitas, chips & salsa, burgers, curry and best of all, very very cold beers.

Cafe 43, 43 Tran Cao Van. This place has the usual traveler fare with Biere Lerue for 10k and bia hoi (pronounced doy in the South) fresh beer for 3000. The food is general traveler fare but tasty. Try the Cao Lao noodles which is the local speciality; the portion size is good. The "fresh spring rolls" (steamed) are around 40k but are huge. This place is becoming more and more popular, in which case Cafe 41 next door may provide an appropriate alternative.

Lantern Town Restaurant, 49 Nguyen Thai Hoc, Hoi An, Vietnam, + 84 1239912212. Hoian is the home of lanterns and Lantern Town restaurant housed in an ancient house combines French colonial architectural influences with traditional Vietnamese style. 80-300 000 dong.

31 Nguyen Thai Hoc Street. Here you can find many small stands which serve good and cheap food quickly.The pick of these is Hi Restaurant, half way down the street. Consistently excellent food at very good prices. The bill is always totalled and detailed correctly too- several local eateries make deliberate errors!! VND25/30,000 upwards.

Bale Well restaurant, 45-51 D Tran Cao Van. Busy in the evenings, less so at lunchtime. Set menu: Bánh Xèo, pork savoury pancakes - Barbecued Satay pork loin, wrap in a lettuce leaf, with side salad veggies. Enjoy with a local beer. Located off the road, up a side alley, beware of the restaurant with similar name facing the street. (January 2014) 90,000 - 110,000 dong.

Blue Dragon. A restaurant by the waterfront with cheap, but good food. Choose from a wide variety of local dishes, or set menus, including meat, vegetarian or seafood choices. A portion of the proceeds goes to help the Blue Dragon Children's Foundation. 40000 dong.

Cafe Bobo, 18 Le Loi. Popular and reasonably-priced. The frappucino-style mocha shakes are great.

Huu Nghi, 56 Bach Dang, 05103910118. Very good food at reasonable prices, with a view of the river and the market. Set meals with 3 or 4 kinds of local specialities for 40.000/70.000 Dong respectively. Fresh beer (Bia Hoi) for 5000 Dong. They also provide a free tiny cup of caramel/vanilla yogurt for dessert.

Laugh Cafe, 126 Tran Cao Van St., Hoi An. Laugh Cafe is a low key Cafe with great, cheap traditional food. It provides vocational training for young people in the provinces surrounding Hoi An, to help give them future opportunities in hospitality. The manager Peter is a laugh (no pun intended) and is happy to have a chat with you about anything you want.

Rosie's Cafe, 8/6 Nguyen Thi Minh Khai. A lovely cafe tucked in a peaceful alley of Nguyen Thi Minh Khai. Signature drink is cold-brew coffee which is less acid than hot brewing and cold pressed juice. Not only the food and drink, but also the space to relax and enjoy the atmosphere of Hoi An old town. 20,000-70,000.

Streets, 17 Le Loi, : +84 (0) 510 3911 948, . till late evening. Well managed social profit café-restaurant offering training and jobs to former street kids. Good food! 150.000.

Pho Ha Noi, 448 Cua Dai Road, 0907269123. Early/Breakfast. The real deal. Pho and bun. Popular with locals. Try out your Vietnamese - limited English understood here. 20000 dong.

Pho Xua, 35 Phan Chau Trinh, Hoi An, Vietnam, 0903112237. Off the main tourist strip, this quiet restaurant offers a very high quality and delicious traditional Vietnamese noodle menu at far lower prices than most other restaurants in the town. The staff are professional, very friendly. The Pho is served with sliced green papaya and kalamansi in addition to the regular side additions and a house potato-chili sauce, making it one of the most unique pho experiences in Hoi An. 30-35k.

Restaurant 96. One of the numerous restaurants by the river banks, this restaurant is packed every night of the week. Many of the guests are returning customers, so the food must be good. There are plenty of vegetarian options and excellent spring rolls. The wait for food tends to be longer than normal, but it's worth it. However the surliness of the owner does affect the general dining experience. 20000 dong.

Thanh Phuong, 56 Cong Dong (An Hoi island, just across bridge and to the left). Standard local fare. A steaming seafood hotpot for two and a large beer will set you back US$9. (As on 18.01.2013 the seafood hotpot is 300.000 Dong. Codfish hotpot 200.000 Dong)

Trung Bac, 87 Tran Phu. 100 years of cao lau and still going strong. A bowl of chewy noodles and lots of veggies will set you back all of 25000 dong. Jan 2014 - it's now 50000 dong and the serving size is terrible.

Shop is really taking advantage of its history and compensating on food quality. Doesn't deserve to be listed here too.

Sun Shine, 46 Tran Cao Van Street (Diagonally opposite Phuoc An Hotel), 0510 3916902. 7AM - 11PM. A homey and cheap restaurant run by a very accommodating and friendly Vietnamese family. Serves fresh and home-cooked Vietnamese and Western food. Food is so-and-so, but okay for the price. Prices start at 25000 dong for a delicious bowl of Cau Lau, and a plate of 6 spring rolls will only set you back 30000 dong. 3000 dong for fresh beer and Vietnamese ice tea is free of charge. As of September 2011, proprietor Hoi is offering cooking lessons for 120,000 dong per person, plus the actual cost of the menu items you wish to prepare (items not on the menu also can be taught). Lessons are fun and instructive; also, the lesson takes place in the house kitchen behind the restaurant, giving you an insight into Vietnamese town life with Hoi and family.

White Lotus, 11 Phan Boi Chau, Hoi An, Vietnam (walk along the river from Old Town, through the central market, and straight on for about 50m, after passing Brother's *Cafe*), 0510 3501009. New restaurant with Australian owner opposite Ha An hotel. Serves good Asian and Western dishes, staff very helpful and obliging to any request. 80000-100000 dong.

White Rose, 533 Hai Ba Trung. The shop that actually makes most of the "white rose" dumplings served all around town and if you ask nicely they'll let you try to make them yourself. Open from 07:00 until they run out, usually in the afternoon. (Update 5 Nov 2012, they now charge 70,000 for White Rose and 100,000 for Wonton. Not cheap)

Mister T's, 639 Hai Ba Trung. If you're looking for a late night snack, this is a great place to go. Most shops/banh mi carts, etc close by 11p/12a and food is hard to find after that. Mister T's is a 24-hour convenient store and fast food kitchen. The guys there will make you a made-to-order toasted ham and cheese sandwich for 45,000dong. Also on the menu: hamburger/chicken burger/veggie burger, hot dog, pizza. Those prices went up to about 60,000dong.

Mid-range
Mango Rooms, 111 Nguyen Thai Hoc, : +84 (0) 510 3910 839, . Mango Rooms offers Asian fusion food with innovative flavors made of fresh local products. As an example try the Duck breast marinated in five spices served with bitter-chocolate passion fruit spicy garlic butter sauce. There are also really delicious cocktails made with fresh fruit juices. The atmosphere is very relaxed with a modern, colorful interior design. The owner and chef, Duc Tran, also opened a second restaurant in Hoi An "Mangomango". Prices are rather upscale (maincourses 350.000-550.000), but definitely worth it! 350k-550k.

Enjoy Restaurant 13 Nguyen Phuc Chu. Offers comfort food: Vietnamese Food, French Food, Burger, Ice Cream Bar (57 Flavors) Lavazza Coffee, Mojito with Havana Club. Open Everyday.

Jaspas Beach Club - international dishes in a beachfront environment. The last Saturday of every month they have a fund raiser to help with the establishment of the An Bang surf lifesaving club. Also monthly parties and happy hours.

Alfrescos 83 tran Hung Dao st. ph.0510 3929 707. Offers comfort food: Aussie steaks, pasta, pizza, Mexican, and ribs. Also home/hotel deliver and do a Tuesday, Friday special deal of two for one pizza for delivery.. Shows rugby and Aussie rules football.

Dingo Deli, 277 Cua Dai Road, 0906 552 824. 7.30AM - 7.30PM. This delicatessen offers an extensive selection of gourmet foods through the restaurant and European grocery store. The ambiance, and aroma of brewed coffee is the attraction for travellers ready to find some favourite tastes from home. The sandwiches and nachos are a nice treat. A wooden constructed adventure play ground is open for children to play on and over looks views of paddocks, buffalo and the Thu Bon river.

Vinh Hung 1 Restaurant, 147B Tran Phu Str (Located opposite the Cantonese Assembly Hall, near the Japanese Bridge), . Open daily for breakfast, lunch and dinner. The Vinh Hung Restauant was one of the first restaurants in Hoi An to open it's doors to Western travelers. A restaurant offering dishes using the freshest ingredients, bought market fresh everyday. Located by the beautiful Japanese Bridge in the centre of Hoi An Old Town, it's a fabulous place to relax over a drink and watch the hustle and bustle of life pass by. *Update Jan 2014 The Pho Bo is 70,000 and comes with little meat or flavor. This has become a tourist trap.

Green Chili, 22 Nguyen Thai Hoc, +84(0)510 3928199, . Steaks and burgers off the grill. American and Tex-Mex. Chips & Salsa, Quesadillas, Nachos.

Baby Mustard, Đường Biển, Điện Dương, Tra Que (Located off the main road in Tra Que, look for the sign), 093 572 57 40. Open daily for lunch and dinner, also hosts daily cooking classes. About 5 km away from

Hoi An proper, Baby Mustard takes the concept of "garden-to-table" to a whole other level. They grow their own herbs and vegetables in the back of the restaurant and everything is amazingly fresh and delicious. The rice comes from across the street and even the pepper is made there. Mains are from about 60k-100k and worth every dong. They offer daily cooking classes and you can even ask for a tour of the garden to taste and smell everything you just ate. Cannot recommend highly enough - GO!

Bazar Cafe & Restaurant, 36 Tran Phu, next to the town market, 0510.3911229, . 8.00AM - 12PM. New in the town, serves the best Vietnamese and Merranean Barbeque in the Garden. Comfortable Lounge, Cocktails and Shisha inside the Wooden Traditional House.

Thanh restaurant, 76 Bach Dang (City centre, riverside), 0510.3861366. Great Vietnamese and Western food. Excellent grilled fished in banana leaf and nice river view. A lot of photos of Hoi An to see

River Lounge, 35 Nguyen Phuc Chu, across the bridge on Hoi An Island, it's the first double-storey building on the immediate left., 0510.3911700, . 8.30AM - 12PM. This new and exciting addition to the restaurants of Hoi An, is run by two entrepeneurial Austrian brothers who are bringing excellent tastes and tunes to this historical town. Western/vietnamese fusion food. Set menu for 120,000, 3 course meal....

Hoi An Cruise Restaurant (Romantic Sunset dinner, relaxing dinner cruise and cooking cruise), 76 Bach Dang street (Reservation office at the city centre), 0510.3623777, . Cruise restaurant with a sunset dinner cruise and cooking class.

Casa Verde, 504 Cua Dai street, 0510 3911594, . This invigorating German owned restaurant serves the best pizzas in Hoi An, his expertise comes from years of experience, as head chef of the Victoria Hotel. Much of the homemade ice cream in Hoi An comes from his kitchen. Fantastic salads. Note: 99 Bach Dang street was his old location years ago and is now Nhà Y Casa Italia, whose pizzas are $2 cheaper. 130k. .

Morning Glory, 106 Nguyen Thai Hoc, +84 510 224 1555, . Choose from a variety of local dishes, and be sure to experiment, because everything is truly excellent. The staff speak good English, the place is beautifully decorated, and the food will have you coming back for more. (And if you really enjoy the food, ask about their cooking classes.) While there are cheaper places to eat in Hoi An, this one is by no means expensive, especially considering how good the food is. Most main courses are between 65,000 and 120,000 dong.

Moon restaurant & lounge, 321 Nguyen Diuy Hieu (East of the market), (+84 510) 2241 396, . 7AM - 10PM. Beautiful old house, laid-back atmosphere and superb Vietnamese food. You can trust the cocktails since it's made of genuine brand spirits, in many other places the hangover can be terrible. main courses 50,000-80,000 drinks 20,000-50,000

Red Bridge Restaurant & Cooking School, Thon 4, Cam Thanh, Hoi An (Catch a meter Taxi, about 3km out of town, cost VND32,000), 0510 933 222, . 10AM - 9PM. Located on the Thu Bon River, The Red Bridge Restaurant and Cooking School offer a wide range of Modern Vietnamese Food, in an open air restaurant. It is set in 2 acres of tropical gardens, and offers a range of tours and clases. Catch a taxi there, or if you have a motorbike or bike just ride, its about 3km. Red Bridge Cooking Classes begin around 8AM at the Hai Scout Cafe for a coffee (Italian Style) then a tour of the market to shop for fruit & veg. a visit to the Organic Herb Farm and a trip up the river in their little red boat to the school. It's funny & fun, eat what you made plus more & relax by the pool with beer & wine. Red Bridge is run by experts- it's a must in Hoian. Booking for dinner are essential, due to the location, they sometimes close early if there are no customers. The food is well priced, and very good value, with large portions, and very good produce. They offer a selection of cocktails as well as the usual beers and an extensive wine list. This is an excellent establishment for an evening meal, especially during sunset.

Son Hoi An, 177 Cua Dai (*Riverside on the Cua Dai beach road*). Very popular stopping point for those cycling back from the beach. Well reviewed.

Brother's Café, 27 - 29 - 31 Phan Boi Chau street, Hoi An ancient town, 84 510 3914150 (, fax: 84 510 3923012). Brother's might be stretching the "mid-range" category. The tranquil French colonial riverside setting is the precursor to a lengthy menu beginning with appetizers of Hoi An special yellow noodle with pork charsjiu & fresh vegetables, Quang Nam white noodle soup with charsjiu pork meat & shrimps, Hoi An "white roses" dumplings, fresh spring rolls, prawns on toast, Hoi An deep -fried special spring rolls, deep-fried wonton, crispy prawn, and crispy calamari. There are five different soups, four salads, five different pork, chicken and beef dishes each (including a grilled pork chop in five flavors sauce), and several sea food entrees. Service is top notch, and the waitresses are invariably cute and demure, yet quite able to explain the different options.

Ganesh Indian Restaurant, 24 Tran Hung Dao, Hoi An, Vietnam (*It is near the corner on Le Loi street, junction of Tran Hung Dao*). Probably the only Indian restaurant and yet very good Indian dishes, e.g. must try their naans and butter chicken! May be suitable for those looking for a restaurant that does not serve pork.

Drink

An Hoi Island, which is the western of the two islands that connect to Old Town, lights up with bars in the evening replete with colorful lanterns and blaring modern pop music. They stay open until after midnight, and cater specifically to the foreign crowd. They are all located on a single strip along the north side of An Hoi overlooking the river, so it is easy to spot which ones are full of people and which ones are more quiet, depending on your social preference.

Sunflower Hostel - Located east of old town and about a 10-15 minute walk, it is primarily a hostel. However, as one of the most popular hostels in Hoi An, it also serves as a drinking venue that is filled with backpackers that want to mingle and drink until the wee hours of the morning.

Casual open-air bars - There are many places to casually drink in quiet, relaxed venues all over Old Town. In particular, along the south end of Le Loi street, and all along Nguyễn Thái Học street are many of these types of bars. Mango, Tam Tam, Q Bar, Before and Now, are examples of bars along these streets that seem to be slightly more occupied than others (at least in the off season).

Volcano Club - a rather empty club (at least in July 2014) that is situated on the north side of Old Town, but is one of the few drinking establishments that is a club rather than a bar.

Why Not? Bar - a small bar located on the east side of town.

Zero Sea Mile Bar - while blogs on the internet sing the praises of this nightclub that oversees the Cua Dai beach (and according to several false reports of it temporarily being closed for renovations but now open), it has been permanently closed and is no longer in existence as of July 2014. Despite conflicting information on the internet, its closure has been verified in person by and no replacement venue has taken its place. In other words, there are no discotheques in the beach area, as Zero Sea Mile is touted as being the one and only. Don't believe any locals that tell you otherwise, as some still genuinely believe it is still in existence based on heresay.

Cafe Bonsai - The place seems more about growing bonsais but for me they had the best Vietnamese coffee in town. You find it going South East on Đinh Tiên Hoàng, it is about 70 meters (left hand) after the intersection with Hai Bà Trưng.

The End

www.ingramcontent.com/pod-product-compliance
Lightning Source LLC
Chambersburg PA
CBHW031108080526
44587CB00011B/881